OtherWise Christian

OtherWise Christian:
A Guidebook for Transgender Liberation

By Mx. Chris Paige

OtherWise Engaged Publishing

First edition July 2019
Forward by the Rev. Louis Mitchell
Cover and cover photo by Chris Paige
Author photo by Dezjorn Gauthier

ISBN: 978-1-951124-00-7 (Paperback)
ISBN: 978-1-951124-03-8 (Large Print)
ISBN: 978-1-951124-01-4 (Kindle)
eISBN: 978-1-951124-02-1

Published by OtherWise Engaged Publishing
http://otherwiseengaged.wordpress.com

Visit http://www.otherwisechristian.com

This book is dedicated
to OtherWise prophets,
past, present, and future,
who have taught me so much:

in memory of Bobbie Jean Baker and
Charlene Arcila,

in memory of Audre Lorde and
Leslie Feinberg,

in honor of Miss Major Griffin-Gracy,
Jonathon Thunderword, and
Kate Bornstein,

with thanksgiving for Nevaeh Paige,
Ovid Amorson, and
all of the Young Leaders,
transgender and OtherWise,
who are yet to come.

CONTENTS

Forward

OtherWise Christian, much like Transfaith, was born of a need for something that did not already exist. I have known them for nearly a decade and Chris Paige is a bit of a spiritual mid-wife—giving birth to new life in a variety of ways. Chris has a knack both for identifying critical needs and for finding the adjacent opportunities waiting nearby.

I am not an authority on all things biblical, but I do live in a world that often uses Christian teachings and texts to erase, disable, disparage, and demean me. I have a stake in this conversation because, as a Black transgender Christian, I nurse the bruises and count the scars of my various religious experiences. Yet, I find comfort more and more in the embrace of God—as I experience the All in my life. Like many of my friends and colleagues I am deeply invested in exploring, engaging, and even wrestling with the words of our ancestors in faith. I am both spiritual and religious, and this book gives me plenty to work with and work on.

I have spent time with many books and scholars, seminaries and Bible studies, reading, searching and listening for deeper, more nuanced ways to engage with biblical texts. I finally found what I was looking for and more in this book! I actually wept with joy a few times as I read.

One of the hardest things about being a Christian believer in modernity (or at any time, I imagine) is that we are discouraged from arguing with, wrestling with, dancing with—we are discouraged from having an honest relationship with the Bible. We have been fed interpretations, and unless we have read them in their original languages and studied the contexts in which they were written, we don't acknowledge (or even know) that we are ingesting someone else's biased understandings. We have taken in all manner of assumptions as "gospel" truth. Yet, these "truths" are not as well founded as they may seem at first glance.

In these pages, Chris Paige has done some initial digging for us—perhaps connecting dots we have always wondered about or maybe just pointing out that there are even dots there to be considered. Weaving together the works of other writers and scholars with their own analyses, Chris has given us a provocative tour through time, space, study, and narrative. *OtherWise Christian* provides a menu of sorts—explorations and queries more than answers or solutions. It is an invitation to continue seeking instead of resting on old ideas. Finally, I have a trans-affirming biblical resource that is clear, to the point, and accessible!

In the time I have known Chris, they have had the courage to be OtherWise in every area of their life: questioning, re-evaluating, wrestling, arguing, reconfiguring, and adjusting—all the stuff that makes most of us uncomfortable and that also allows us to deepen our faith and to grow as people. Not only does this book challenge those who are cisgender to be more trans inclusive, it also challenges those of us who are transgender but also deeply entrenched in the binary.

In their preface, Chris says they aren't a "pastor or priest, neither... theologian nor professor," but I disagree! In these pages, I have found deep pastoral care, powerful ministry, profound spiritual thought, and insightful teaching. When Chris asked me to write this forward, I felt honored and pleased. Yet, as I continued to read, my feelings shifted and exploded beyond mere pleasant connection. Page after page, chapter after chapter, I felt seen, taught, explored, and engaged with. From the exploration of what it might look like to have a "safer spirituality," to the depth and breadth of a "genderfull" Christ, to the lagniappe of reminders that I am loved, every chapter and section offered a salve to my heart.

I find myself motivated to study more and further after reading this book—to question what I thought I knew about the Bible and what it says about gender. I am excited to revisit familiar characters and narratives with a new OtherWise lens. This is an extraordinary gift to the trans community and to those, whether transgender or cisgender, who wish to go deeper in the texts to see those of us who have been hidden, erased, and/or disparaged. Chris is my bestie and I am biased, but that doesn't mean that I am wrong!

There's a passage in the Big Book of Alcoholics Anonymous that bubbled up for me when reading this book. It stems from the ever-present feelings of aloneness in the world of religion, even in "affirming" religious settings. It says,

> There is no more aloneness, with that awful ache, so deep in the heart of every alcoholic, that nothing, before, could ever reach it. That ache is gone and never need return again. Now there is a sense of belonging, of being wanted and needed and loved. In return for a bottle and a hangover, I have been given the Keys of the Kingdom. (*Alcoholics Anonymous*, page 276)

I feel less alone after reading *OtherWise Christian.* I feel seen, sought, valued... and LOVED. It is my hope and prayer that this book lands in every progressive seminary, every house of worship that seeks to understand and embrace the deep diversity of God's creation, and in libraries where our young people may find it.

May every word of this book be a blessing to those of us whose lives often hang precariously on the margins.

Thank you, Chris Paige, for your courageous exploration and witness!

The Rev. Louis J. Mitchell
June 2019

Preface

During times of trouble
I called on the LORD.
The LORD answered me
[and] set me free
[from all of them].

Psalm 118:5
God's Word translation

I offer myself, not as pastor or priest, neither as theologian nor professor. If anything, I am an "Irreverend," who is seeking to disrupt the oppressive ways that even well-meaning Christians talk about transgender liberation. It matters little whether I have studied Latin or Greek (though I did), whether I can properly cite scripture or format a footnote (though I could). What matters most (to me) is that I am a witness to the resurrection. I am a witness to the wisdom and resilience of my people. That commitment is at the core of this book.

I offer myself as a fellow traveler, interested in journeying with you for a little ways through these pages. In *OtherWise Christian: A Guidebook for Transgender Liberation*, I hope to share from what I have learned over twenty years as a transgender and non-binary organizer of European descent and Christian upbringing. I write with thanksgiving for the many gifts I have been given by others on this journey. I write as a way to pass along the generosity that I have received.

If this book helps an ally or accomplice to gain some perspective, then I welcome it. However, I write primarily for my trans siblings, for my intersex cousins, for my non-binary and gender non-conforming kindred, and for all who resist the reductive ideas about gender that so many of us have been taught in the Western world. I write in praise and gratitude for all those who are OtherWise in all our shapes and sizes, all our manifestations and traditions. May past, present, and future join hands as we hold close our ancestors and the elders who have gone before us, our children and the young ones who are yet to come. May each of us know the joy of this lineage that we share.

OtherWise Christian is a love letter to transgender communities, a self defense manual against Bible abuse and Christian trans-antagonism, and the beginning of a historical record of how far we have come. It is an offering of love for my companions and comrades in the struggle because we are worthy, because we are beloved, and because we belong to one another.

A Love Letter

Too many people of transgender experience have had to travel this road alone. Even after finding community that seems to care, many of us go through seasons of feeling abandoned and wandering in the wilderness. In twenty years of organizing among transgender people, I have found no more important resource for transgender people than our finding one another in the fierce tenderness of friendship and community.

The world finds a plethora of ways to tell us that we are unworthy of love, even when we know better. Christianity is particularly known for casting judgment and condemnation. It is a powerful practice for us to remember that Love remains with us at all times. After the 2016 Republican National Convention (in the United States), I started writing "You Are Loved" posts on my Facebook page as a form of resistance. These simple daily reminders seemed to land in a raw spot for many of my friends—especially those of transgender experience.

With that in mind, each chapter of *OtherWise Christian* will include some sort of short reminder that you are loved, that you are valuable, that you are worthy, and that you are not alone. No matter what you may be going through right now, please take a moment to breath in that loving care at each opportunity.

♡

May our children know hope. May our elders know dignity. May our ancestors draw near. You are loved.

A Self-Defense Manual

In many ways, I learned the Bible as a form of self-defense in the 1990s as the "religious right" came into the mainstream. We live in a world where the language and traditions of Christianity are too often used as weapons against people of transgender experience, not only in church settings but also in legislatures, in social media, and even at family gatherings.

Often the weapons used are actually little more than outdated, ill-informed cultural assumptions and "alternative facts" that have nothing to do with "what the Bible says" at all! *OtherWise Christian* provides practical biblical literacy to equip and support our people. The Christian Bible is actually full of an amazing array of gender-diverse characters doing God's work in the world. I invite you to celebrate their testimonies with me.

Where possible, I will also point toward where you can find more in-depth scholarship and/or expanded reflection (especially when I can give recognition to those who labored to bring us these insights). However, in aiming for a brief and accessible starting point, I will leave detailed scholarly arguments for other writers who can afford such luxuries.

That said, more rigorous scholarship would reveal that there is no singular definitive interpretation of any text. There are only the stories that we tell about the stories that we hear about the stories that we read. This is especially true of writings that span more than two millennia, multiple original languages, and the disparate worldviews of at least two major world religions. I certainly concede that alternative interpretations exist, though I am not motivated to argue about it. That said, if I am ever pressed to choose among orthodoxy, academic rigor, and life-giving inspiration, I choose Life.

All this to say that I am not at all concerned with somehow making you a "proper" Christian or convincing you of the "proper" form of Christianity. It is fine with me if you disagree with the options I offer here. I trust you to make your own informed assessment and look forward to what future generations of OtherWise-gendered people may bring to the conversation. Yet, in the short-term, I want to make sure that trans-affirming Christian interpretations of scripture, such as these, get at least as much airtime as the trans-antagonistic alternatives that are so often hurled at our people. We deserve to be well-armed when facing opposition from those who wish us harm.

♡

May the Love of God guide us. May the Living Christ inspire us. May the Holy Spirit move through us. You are loved.

Historical Reference

When I began exploring my gender identity in 1998, I was well-connected to national lesbian and gay Christian organizing across several denominations. I reached out to many of those LGBT organizations for resources and turned up almost nothing that related specifically to transgender experience. The most extensive Christian resources I came across at that time were published by a cardiologist named Rebecca Allison, MD. The most relevant transgender books I could find were from Kate Bornstein and Leslie Feinberg, writing from a primarily secular perspective (though both Jewish in background). The only prominent transgender religious leader I could identify was the Rev. Erin Swenson, who had recently transitioned from male to female and retained her Presbyterian clergy ordination in the Atlanta area.

It is hard to overstate how little material on transgender religious experience was available, even from the far left. Except perhaps in hidden informal enclaves, there were no transgender religious books, no transgender religious organizations, no networks of transgender religious leaders, no events dealing with transgender religious issues. There were just starting to be a few individuals, almost exclusively volunteers, sharing from their own experience.

For my part, I gathered what resources I was able to find and detailed them on a free Angelfire website called *Transfaith Online.* I asked LGBT Christian organizations to link to the resulting resource. *Transfaith Online* would eventually become the #1 Google search result for "transgender Christian." At the time, I did not know that I was knee-deep in what I have come to call the "transgender spring" (from 1996 to 2006) in Christian organizing, as transgender religious voices began to blossom.

Unfortunately, most of that early history is already obscured, if not erased, as transgender communities have been swept up in a world of terribly short-attention spans and an opportunistic non-profit industrial complex. Yet, this book is very much indebted to that community of friends and colleagues, elders and ancestors, path-makers and ground-breakers. *OtherWise Christian* seeks to capture at least a little bit of that important Christian (and Jewish) history, through this book as well as my companion blog (http://www.otherwisechristian.com).

♡

May we remember that we have already come a long way. Come what may, let us not forget one another, nor the grace that has brought us together. You are loved.

Beloved, like these many others before me, I offer you my despair and weariness, my defiance and my resolve, my love and my encouragement as we face this world together. There will be ample time later to review credentials, check footnotes, negotiate politics, defend the faith, find middle ground, repair the breach, and build bridges. There will be time for us to compromise.

But, first let us dream our dreams, rejoice in our gifts, take time for healing, claim our communities, and dance in defiance. Only then will we be truly ready to face all the world has in store for us. If nothing else, I hope you remember this: We do not need their permission—to exist, to sing, to dance, to love, to survive, or to read, write, and interpret. We are already here. We have existed since the beginning of time. We are extraordinary. We are powerful. We have so much Wisdom to offer.

Amen. Blessed be. Thanks be to God.

Mx. Chris Paige

Related Resources

Transfaith at http://www.transfaith.info
OtherWise Christian at http://www.otherwisechristian.com
Rebecca Allison at http://www.drbecky.com/grace.html
Kate Bornstein at http://katebornstein.com
Leslie Feinberg at http://www.lesliefeinberg.net
Erin Swenson at https://erinswenson.com

Introduction

OtherWise Christian: A Guidebook for Transgender Liberation is a love letter to transgender communities, a self defense manual against Bible abuse and Christian trans-antagonism, and the beginning of a historical record of how far we have come. My hope is that it can be used far and wide as a resource for people of transgender experience and those who love us.

At the beginning of each chapter is a short biblical text (and sometimes two). These texts serve to focus the chapter. Some are a primary text for the chapter that follows, and others are simply evocative—offered as an encouraging entry point for the reader. I have used a wide variety of English translations, based on what I believe best represents the text as I am approaching it. Some translations are less well-known than others, but all of the translations are available on the internet for your further exploration. I recommend https://biblehub.com and https://www.blueletterbible.org for those who are interested in further exploring the variations between and among English translations.

Each chapter is relatively brief, though some longer chapters have smaller sub-sections with their own headings. Check the bibliography for resources that can assist with more in-depth reflection on specific claims. The appendices include some additional recommendations and resources. You may also want to check out the *OtherWise Christian* companion blog at http://www.otherwisechristian.com, where I will share more details and links, book reviews, and historical reflections.

OtherWise Christian should read well from front to back like a novel, if you want to be orderly about it. However, it is also designed to be used as a reference, like a dictionary or an encyclopedia, so you can jump to whatever topic you need most in the moment. The chapters are grouped into sections so that closely related content can be more easily accessed. In many chapters, I also provide "see also" notes to help you find additional chapters where particular topics are discussed. So feel free to jump around according to your interests.

Between the short attention span of social media networks and the mechanics of the LGBT non-profit industrial complex, even the most recent history of transgender Christians is increasingly obscured. With *OtherWise Christian*, I also seek to bear witness to the path-makers and ground-breakers who have brought us this far. I highlight certain authors and publications, because I believe that it is important for us to remember our history. A lot has happened in the last 25 years! May we remember these leaders and their contributions with joy and thanksgiving.

Some of my early readers have had emotional reactions to some of the topics that I raise. That is ok! At the bottom of each chapter, you will find a "You are loved" statement. Whatever your reactions are, please give yourself a few moments to breathe in those messages of love. A book like this is about both feelings and knowledge, wisdom and resilience. If a "You are loved" statement does not work for you, then I hope you will rewrite and reframe it in some way that is useful to you. Yes, I am inviting you to write in the book—only not if it is borrowed from someone else!

In many ways, this is the initial quick reference that I would have loved to find when I first started exploring my gender identity as a twenty-something Christian, so I am especially interested in reaching **campus ministries, LGBT student groups, and transgender support groups**. I even applied for funding from three different agencies that support transgender people. I asked them to support a targeted distribution of books to those populations. All three funders declined saying they did not understand why sharing this book would be important.

- If you think that *OtherWise Christian* should be in the hands of as many young people, student groups, and new in transition people as want to receive it, then please drop me a note to **let me know why you think it is important.**

- If you are interested in sharing *OtherWise Christian* with others, please reach out to me directly to discuss **subsidies for orders of 5 or more books** that will reach those populations.

- If you are someone who is interested in helping the next generation of leaders to benefit from this survey of trans-affirming biblical reflection, then please contact me or go to my website to **support those subsidies**.

Find me at otherwise.christian@gmail.com or http://www.otherwisechristian.com. I would love to hear from you!

Whether you are a devoted Christian, someone struggling to figure out your relationship with Christianity (or transgender communities), or just someone who wants to be better able to defend themselves from the trans-antagonistic Christians around you, my prayer is that you will find company in these pages to support your journey.

♡

Greetings! You are loved. When you are lonely. When you are seeking. You are not sure what community you belong to. You are loved.

Abbreviations

Most abbreviations are spelled out in the text, except the following:

CEV Contemporary English Version
KJV King James Version
NKJV New King James Version
NIV New International Version

SECTION ONE
Getting Started

Chapter 1
Practicing Safer Spirit/uality (Choose Life)

I am now giving you the choice
between life and death,
between God's blessing
and God's curse,
and I call heaven and earth
to witness the choice you make.
Choose life.

Deuteronomy 30:19
Good News Translation

Ideas about "practicing safer spirit/uality" are a useful jumping-off point for our conversation about transgender liberation. In a world that has been so deeply colonized by reductive notions about gender, we find that all too often conversations about gender (and sexuality) begin defensively—trying to prove that we are who we say we are, that we should be allowed to exist, that we are not somehow inherently dangerous.

However, if our ultimate goal is liberation then we need to do more than simply defend certain Western experiences of gender as acceptable within a Christian context. In order to be liberated, we must identify the source of that which binds us and begin to dismantle its influence on us. In other words, we need to talk about why we were ever forced to defend ourselves in the first place. What are the dynamics that make Christian spirituality so unsafe for so many transgender people? And how do we practice a safer spirit/uality?

Chris Glaser and Marvin Ellison have both offered up ideas on "Practicing Safer Spirit/uality." Their language riffs off "safer sex" practices and precautions in the Western world. Like sexuality, spirituality is both potentially beautiful and empowering as well as potentially dangerous and alienating. Both Glaser and Ellison define spiritual abuse and go on to provide insights about how we might protect ourselves.

In Chris Glaser's 1998 chapter titled, "Practicing Safer Spirit," he writes about spiritual abuse:

> Spiritual abuse may be practiced from the pulpit to the Sunday school classroom, from the family home to the television airwaves. Spiritual abuse is experienced when we are treated as less than children of God or told we are not made in the image of God. Spiritual abuse is experienced when our souls are manipulated, tortured, or enslaved by the threat of hellfire, excommunication, or abandonment. (Glaser, 1998 edition, pages 29–30)

In Marvin Ellison's 2009 chapter titled, "Practicing Safer Spirituality: Changing the Subject and Focusing on Justice," he also tackles "religiously legitimated oppression or unsafe spirituality, [and]... spiritual abuse" (Ellison, page 8). Ellison draws on the work of Karen Lebacqz and Joseph Driskill to outline a typical pattern for spiritual abuse:

> [A] powerful person assumes that his or her authority is sacrosanct and beyond question; a more vulnerable party is made to feel inadequate and shamed; and the powerful party encourages defining the problem as the vulnerable one who must be "saved," "fixed," or expelled from the community if recalcitrant. (Ellison, page 8)

Glaser offers individual spiritual practices as a "spiritual prophylactic" against spiritual abuse. Ellison takes a more systemic approach, suggesting that a reformation of the Christian tradition itself is a necessary corrective, a "*transformation*, a dismantling of hierarchical social power and of the patriarchal conceptual framework that legitimates gender and sexual oppression" (Ellison, page 7). Ok. I know that was way more 3+ syllable words in a row than many of us would prefer! To put it more simply, Glaser is talking about how individuals can protect themselves, and Ellison is talking about how systems and institutions and culture need to change to stop putting people at risk.

Glaser and Ellison write as cisgender gay men, but it is worth noting that their reckoning with the dynamics of spiritual abuse may resonate yet more deeply for transgender communities. Transgender people have been thoroughly subjected to a variety of powerful authorities who have sought to regulate both our identities and our access to basic human resources. Such authorities, including medical professionals, mental health professionals, legal professionals, and government officials, are often pragmatically referred to as "gatekeepers."

In the realm of Christianity, religious professionals in both the church and the academy have played a similar role, serving as gatekeepers and magistrates in a variety of ways. While there are plenty of good reasons to have systems of leadership and accountability within the institutional church, there is also ample evidence that such authority has been used to maintain the status quo, to discredit prophetic voices, and to otherwise ignore vital movements of the Spirit in our midst. The academy has its own rhetoric of "higher learning," which prides itself on detached objectivity and peer review, but scholars immersed in those institutions can be even more insular than church folk.

To put *OtherWise Christian* into context, it is important to understand that religious gatekeepers, no matter how well meaning, remain a part of a larger system that is largely unrepentant in its efforts to control and manage transgender people. Indeed, transgender people have been perpetually treated as patients to be fixed, clients to be served, issues to be discussed, problems to be solved, and threats to be managed. This "defining the problem" dynamic deployed against transgender people is also the typical pattern for spiritual abuse that was outlined by Ellison.

It is relatively rare that transgender people are treated as experts on our own lived experience. This is a problem, which has a variety of harmful impacts insofar as people with less experience and less investment regularly make authoritative decisions on behalf of those of us with the most at stake. This system of disempowerment leads directly to spiritual abuse as the agency and self-determination of transgender people is so frequently and consistently challenged. The submission that is required by these outside authorities in order to gain access to basic human resources has a lingering effect.

An entire book could be written exploring the role of condescension in the behaviors of gatekeepers toward transgender people, but that is not my priority here. I will simply offer that after 20 years at the bleeding edge of transgender Christianity, I have been disappointed in the ability of both the church and the academy to prioritize transgender wellness with consistency and integrity. No matter how well-meaning or insightful the conversations might sometimes be, the apparatus of these institutions is designed for exclusivity, not accessibility. In my experience, neither church nor academy has proved to be trustworthy nor sacrosanct authorities when it comes to transgender wellness.

So, my most important plumb line for *OtherWise Christian* has to do with whether transgender lives are being centered, whether transgender experience is being valued, whether transgender wellness is being served. In what ways are clergy folk invested in the survival of transgender communities? Does academic discourse make a difference in the lives of transgender people who are struggling? Is it reasonable for us to submit ourselves to authorities who, at best, equivocate about whether they can accept our insights and testimonies (or, at worst, tell us that we are wrong, sick, and sinful)?

To put it bluntly, safer (transgender) spirituality means trusting transgender people. I believe, first and foremost, that transgender people are experts on our own lives. I believe that transgender people typically ask (and answer) deeply spiritual questions as a matter of course, such as "Who am I? How do I fit into this world? Why am I here?" I believe that transgender people develop transferable skills that serve us well in the realm of spiritual discernment. It is my lived experience that there is no more important resource for transgender survival than our relationships with other transgender people.

That said, I certainly trust transgender people to read scripture for ourselves. While I respect the traditions of the church and the scholarship of academics as sometimes useful resources, the fact is that those fields rarely reflect or include transgender leaders. Those transgender leaders who function in their midst testify to the cost they bear for that access. These are fields that have been colonized by trans-antagonistic forces for centuries now, and the supposed "objectivity" of such studies actually protects bias against us while actively preventing the kind of open, honest, heartfelt engagement and empathy that would allow for deep transformation.

Rather than begging for approval from such institutions, I have increasingly turned to the testimonies of prophets, to those who contribute to the survival and liberation of our people by bravely and courageously breaking the rules, flipping the script, claiming our lives as our own. For transgender people, safer spirituality necessarily means choosing the wisdom of our people over that of external authorities. Safer spirituality means choosing life-affirming practices over negotiations with allegedly disinterested systems of knowledge. Safer spirituality means choosing Life over Death, liberation over submission.

With *OtherWise Christian*, I choose Life. Again and again, I choose Life. I hope that you will join me.

♡

You are loved. When you trust yourself and your lived experience. When you trust your people and their Wisdom. When you defy those who demand your submission. You are loved.

Chapter 2
On (OtherWise) Transgender Liberation

Beloved ones,
God has called us
to live a life of freedom
in the Holy Spirit.

Galatians 5:13a
The Passion Translation

I use the word "transgender" in this book and in my organizing out of convenience as a broad (and imperfect) umbrella term, while recognizing that the specific language our people use for ourselves is varied, creative, powerful, and embedded in living communities and unique cultural contexts. Best practices in transgender education typically define "transgender" as something like what Merriam Webster (Online 2019) says, "of, relating to, or being a person whose gender identity differs from the sex the person had or was identified as having at birth."

Honestly, the conversation about gender terminology is a large, challenging, and rapidly evolving project of its own. As I write this, some alternative umbrella phrases include "transgender and gender non-conforming" or "transgender and non-binary" in an effort to expand the conversation more intentionally beyond binary notions of "male to female" and "female to male" transsexual or transgender experience. Intersex is now sometimes being added to the "LGBT" acronym, though awareness and understanding of the unique needs and experiences of intersex people vary widely. "Transgender and intersex" is another variation that seeks to acknowledge the limitations of "transgender" as an umbrella term.

Yet, even these well-meaning options hedge on questions of race, religion, culture, and language by continuing to allow limited Western conceptions of sex and gender to define the field of conversation. The project of transgender liberation must necessarily interrogate that brutal legacy of settler-colonial violence that has shaped and continues to shape the ways that most North American Christians think about both gender and liberation.

To put it another way, colonization is not just something that "happened" to Native Americans several hundred years ago. It is a powerful and influential worldview that continues to thrive and adapt in the contemporary world. The ideology that claims there are two and only two mutually exclusive gender identities (male and female) is closely tied to European (and Christian) settler-colonist values—which in turn align with the violence of white supremacy and Christian supremacy.

Jewish tradition, Christian tradition, and hundreds of indigenous cultures testify to more sophisticated and nuanced understandings of the diversity of God's gender-full creation. Even Western science has shown that biological sex is not as simple as we have been led to believe—and the testimonies of intersex people help us to comprehend the many surprising ways that reproductive organs, chromosomes, hormones, and secondary sex markers can come together to form delightful and brilliant human beings.

Western, settler-colonist gender ideology is essentially a religious assertion. If you are committed to the notion that there are two and only two mutually exclusive, permanent, and unchanging genders, then little I write or say will convince you *OtherWise*. Within that framework, transgender and intersex people are simply "broken." At best, you may carve out slightly more spacious corners in your worldview to accommodate a more compassionate approach to those who deviate from your expectations.

If you hold such prior assumptions, then it is only natural that you will also read those assumptions back into the ancient world as narrated by the Christian Bible. Yet, that Bible was not written by European Christians intent on subduing and controlling a world full of "savages" and "deviants." Both Hebrew and Greek texts were written long before "Manifest Destiny" and the "Doctrine of Discovery" gave European Christians self-absorbed rationales to justify invasions, enslavement, and genocide of various indigenous peoples.

In the context of colonized North American Christianity, it is easy to forget that we are reading Western conceptions of sex and gender back into the lives of people who lived 2,000 (or more) years ago on another continent with a different worldview. However, this Christian (and Jewish) sacred text also supports our resistance. Indeed, the Christian Bible is full of stories of God's strengthening resilience and resistance among nomads and slaves, farmers and fisherfolk who faced slavery, exploitation, and colonization (from Egypt to the Roman occupation).

OtherWise Christian invites us to read the Christian Bible and the development of Christian traditions with some historical context, while grappling with the ways colonization continues to shape our thinking about sex, gender, race, and religion. Efforts toward transgender liberation will necessarily have limited impact when they fail to embrace in full measure these traditions of resilience and resistance. This means that we must question again and again the ways that our language and pre-existing ideas may shape the way we perceive both the world and the text.

I will use "OtherWise-gendered" to mean "any gender identity or expression that transcends the simplistic Western settler-colonist narrative of two and only two mutually exclusive and unchangeable genders, defined strictly and easily based on biology at birth." 'OtherWise-gendered people" includes both modern "transgender" people as defined by Merriam Webster as well as some (not all!) modern intersex people. However, the definition here has to do with resisting or transcending Western settler-colonist gender ideology, rather than suggesting that transgender and intersex experience are the same. Meanwhile, "OtherWise-gendered" also stretches to embrace gender identities and expressions that are based in other cultures, worldviews, and understandings (for example, two spirit, *fa'afafine*, *waria*, *muxe*, *hijra*, etc).

When I say "OtherWise-gendered," I am pointing to the wisdom and insight of a gender-full resistance. I am pointing to the many kinds of people whose life experiences have been trampled on or confined by Western, settler-colonist assumptions and ideology. As such, it is important to be clear that OtherWise-gendered is not a singular experience or way of being. Rather, OtherWise-gendered is an effort to open the doors and the windows to make more space for us to listen earnestly to the diversity of God's good creation in all its many gender-full forms.

♡

You are loved. When they refuse your gifts. When they get it twisted. When they use your story to cause harm. You are loved.

Chapter 3
Gender Diversity in Historical Context

If the people of this world
hate you,
just remember
that they hated me first.

John 15:18
Contemporary English Version
(said by Jesus)

Let us be clear. OtherWise-gendered people are nothing new. Clearly, the modern English words we use to talk about gender are new and rapidly evolving, so it is not fair to say that "transgender people" as defined by Merriam Webster in 2019 have always existed. However, language and customs around gender have always varied by culture and tradition.

Indigenous people in cultures around the world have acknowledged and affirmed identities such as *fa'afafine*, *waria*, *muxe*, *hijra*, *mashoga*, and many more. These words are not interchangeable. Each term represents a gender-full identity unique to and embedded in its particular cultural context.

Meanwhile, in what we now call North America, the English term, "two spirit," has been used as an umbrella term to express solidarity among the diverse array of more specific culturally based identities such as *nádleehí*, *winkté*, *niizh manidoowag*, *hemaneh*, *nde'isdzan*, *asegi*, and *badé*. Even though two spirit is used as an umbrella term, there has never been a generic or universal two spirit identity. Like other identities from around the world, each identity is deeply intertwined with a specific culture and language.

In fact, two spirit is an important example of how "umbrella terms" fail. The phrase "two spirit" is a direct translation of the Ojibwe term, *niizh manidoowag*. It was adopted in 1990 in the third of five North American convenings of indigenous gay and lesbian people. Anthropologists had popularized a French word (that I will not use) which reflected the (offensive) values of colonizers about gender and sexual diversity. Offering "two spirit" as an alternate pan-Native term was a strategic intervention on the part of those most impacted. They wanted to name themselves on their own terms. Yet, the rise of "two spirit" has also served to obscure the existence, not to mention nuance, of many more specific and varied indigenous traditions.

The phrase "two spirit" does not even translate well into certain indigenous languages (and cultural frameworks). For example in Diné (also called Navajo) culture, the *nádleehí* is an effeminate male. *Nádleehí* means "changing one" and it is a fluid identity. A *nádleehí* may express themselves differently from one day to the next, embodying either a male or a female role at different times. As such, "two spirit" does not accurately reflect Diné ideas about the *nádleehí*. It is actually misleading. Congruent with its origins, two spirit is more of a pan-Native political intervention than a functional gender identity. To really understand Native ideas about gender requires getting to know more about specific Native cultures and traditions.

Classical Jewish tradition, on which Christianity relies, acknowledges at least 6 different genders (including *androgynos*, *tumtum*, *ay'lonit*, *saris*). Jesus himself shows a gender-full awareness in Matthew 19:12 when he says there are three kinds of eunuchs, meaning he knew of at least three (or five) genders (depending on how you count). I will explore the significance of those comments from Jesus in more detail in chapter 14.

Unfortunately, European Christian colonization around the world has worked for centuries to erase and suppress these gender-full expressions, often through brutal forms of violence. From conquistadors to Christian missionaries, from residential schools to the Bureau of Indian affairs, two spirit people have been specifically targeted for incarceration, torture, and death, if they did not conform to the narrow gender expectations of the European settler-colonists. Similar dynamics occurred in other parts of the world.

That their communities of origin often honored these OtherWise-gendered people as healers, mystics, mediators, and visionaries only made such attacks all the more insidious. Even in less violent times, OtherWise-gendered experiences are often stigmatized, ridiculed, and driven underground. OtherWise-gendered people are often pressured to conform to binary gender expectations in order to receive medical care or legal documentation. Yet, these OtherWise identities and expressions continue to survive and/or erupt, whether affirmed or not.

Such diverse and gender-full language and culture are not simply relics from history, but they persist as OtherWise-gendered people articulate our experiences in each new generation. While survey tools are notorious for collapsing individuality, the landmark 2008 National Transgender Discrimination Survey (NTDS) created space for respondents to write in their own gender if the predefined categories were not representative ("A Gender Not Listed Here").

These write-in survey results included non-binary terms such as genderqueer, androgynous, non-gendered, gender fluid, third gender, and pangender, as well as culturally specific terms such as *mahuwahine*, two spirit, and aggressive (Harrison, et al., page 14). These examples show that a variety of gender language continues to be meaningful within specific cultures (or subcultures), even if it is not universally applicable or even widely understood.

In addition, other terms may erupt along the way as individuals or communities find new words of resistance to articulate their experiences. Results from the NTDS survey also included unique terms including twidget, burl, OtherWise (yes, that was me!), birl, Jest me, skaneelog, neutrois, gendertreyf, trannydyke genderqueer wombat fantastica, Best of Both, and gender blur (Harrison, et al., page 20). Survey respondents were not asked to define these terms, so we simply get to enjoy the creativity that was demonstrated and imagine what these terms might represent. Of course, not every term will catch on widely, but each is nonetheless indicative of the strength and self-determination of OtherWise-gendered people who are claiming their authentic selves in the face of OtherWise-limited options.

The tension between uprisings of gender-full life and the suppression of such expressions is important to understand. This interplay between visibility and invisibility, compliance and non-compliance shapes gender-full communities in profound ways. Language can be used to define, resist, make visible, and empower, but it can just as effectively be used to target, condemn, expel, and oppress. Often the visibility that is required to appear in the public eye or on the historical record comes with significant risk. OtherWise-gendered people typically organize first and foremost for survival, which may or may not include dominant Western models of political organizing. That means our most important and powerful work has often been in private, intimate spaces, and/or at the margins of institutional and public life.

Beware of those who would tell you that gender diversity is something new, that gender diversity is a white, liberal, privileged invention, or even that people of transgender experience are historical late-comers to movements for liberation. We are talking about several centuries of resistance to the violence and erasure embedded in Western settler-colonist ideology. Such resistance is intentionally ignored, erased, or demonized by the powers that be and yet remains ever present for those who have eyes to see and ears to hear (Matthew 13:9–16).

The advent of the internet and social media has brought a major shift in cultural representation. The internet did not invent OtherWise-gendered experiences, but it has provided a game-changing source of both visibility and community conversation. Instead of being isolated by geography, a widespread national and global conversation about gender has emerged in discussion groups, blogs, podcasts, and video. Insofar as the scope of that conversation has drawn attention, particularly from white professional-class folk, it is now seen as more substantive and credible than it was when media production was more centralized and OtherWise-gendered folk lived closer at the margins or in the shadows of mainstream conversation.

Yet, the most visible forms of OtherWise-gendered community are only the tip of the iceberg. They are just that—the most visible forms of OtherWise-gendered community. The most vulnerable networks of OtherWise-gendered community tend to remain more insular for reasons of safety and survival. We persist, even when out of sight, sometimes hidden in plain view, increasingly on the record. Yet, we remain vulnerable to fresh waves of suppression that may drive us underground again.

♡

You are loved. When they try to erase or remove you. When they tell you that you are not supposed to exist. You are loved.

SECTION TWO
Creation

Chapter 4
Sex, Gender, Science, and Arguments from Natural Law

And God saw every thing
that he had made,
and, behold,
it was very good.

Genesis 1:31a KJV

The idea that gender (or sex) have two and only two mutually exclusive options is so deeply embedded in Western society that many call it "obvious" or "common sense." In some circles, this "obvious" may even be framed as "natural law" or "natural theology," which is to say that it is discoverable by reasoned observation (and not dependent on religious revelation).

The history of "natural law" is one that extends over centuries from Plato (5th and 4th century, BCE) to the present. Christian theologians such as Augustine of Hippo, Thomas Aquinas, and C.S. Lewis (among others) developed ideas from Greek and Roman philosophers (and each other) as part of their specifically Christian worldview. This topic extends far beyond sex and gender into issues of theology, law and politics. Published in 2015, Megan DeFranza's *Sex Difference in Christian Theology: Male, Female, and Intersex in the Image of God* offers a helpful survey of ideas about gender from the ancient world to today.

Natural variations of sex and gender, then referred to as "hermaphrodites" and "eunuchs," were a well-known phenomenon in the ancient world (though these terms are not in common use today, and "hermaphrodite" is now considered a slur):

> In the classical world, sex and gender were understood as a ladder of ascent toward perfection. At the top were manly men—understood as the pinnacle not only of male perfection, but also of human perfection. At the bottom were women and children. Unmanly men, hermaphrodites, and eunuchs occupied the middle. (DeFranza, page 114)

According to DeFranza, the ancients thought in hierarchy, not binary. There were not two sexes. There was only a single sex, with a variety of inferior expressions:

> The male existed as the only true sex, the only true human. Women, eunuchs, and hermaphrodites had lesser bodies and, consequently, lesser souls. Their souls were defective in reason and virtue, for virtue was believed to be derived from *vir* (the male). Nevertheless, despite their status as lesser humans, women, eunuchs, and hermaphrodites were usually granted human status and were believed to at least possess some measure of (rational) soul, no matter how deficient. (DeFranza, pages 116--117)

From Aristotle (4th century BCE) to Thomas Aquinas (13th century CE) into the Reformation (16th century CE), the idea that women were simply "defective" or "misbegotten" men ruled the day:

> The early Christian Fathers... found it very easy to accept the pagan beliefs, circulating in Greece and Rome, that the male is the perfect human while women, eunuchs, and hermaphrodites are imperfect, mutilated, misbegotten, or inverted humans. (DeFranza, page 117)

> Physicians in the classical and medieval periods were familiar with hermaphroditic bodies, and while they theorized about their origins, they did not usually attempt to alter them. The management of intersex was more often handled on the familial, legal, and religious levels. Jewish scribes pulled from laws pertaining to men and women to regulate religious and domestic behaviors of hermaphrodites. (DeFranza, page 48)

In other words, there were plenty of genders other than "male" and "female," and they were well integrated into society. However, men were considered the ultimate human expression above all others.

In his 2013 book, *Queering the Ethiopian Eunuch: Strategies of Ambiguity in Acts*, Sean Burke (citing Jonathan Walters) frames this conversation around "men and unmen" (Burke, page 71). He explores the various factors that would qualify (or disqualify) someone as a man (or *vir*). Such dynamics extended far beyond biological features to include age, class, nationality and sexual practice:

> The identity category "men" could be limited to those who were recognized as hard, active, dominant, inviolable, impenetrable, sexually insertive, self-disciplined free adult male citizens or natives. The identity category "unmen" could include women, foreigners, slaves, and children, all of whom were defined as soft, passive, submissive, violable, penetrable, sexually receptive, and ruled by emotions. (Burke, page 71)

In other words, masculinity was not just about gender. It was about power and domination of men over unmen.

According to DeFranza, it was not until the Reformation's emphasis on (heterosexual) marriage as the ideal that a different kind of binary thinking about sex and gender began to take root, emphasizing a polarity between two "opposite" genders:

> By eliminating monasteries and arguing for the normativity of marriage, the Reformers effectively kept all women at home under the rule of husbands with a strict division of labor, and eroded the safe spaces by and for eunuchs during the Middle Ages. This theological and political move laid the groundwork for the hardening of sex differentiation, the elimination of a third sex, and the doctrine of separate spheres that would come to full flower in the Victorian era, but not before it passed through the philosophical revolution of the Enlightenment. (DeFranza, pages 127–128)

In other words, the idea of "two mutually exclusive genders" is something they came up with relatively recently (16th century CE).

DeFranza (following Thomas Laqueur) argues that binary sex, as we know it now, was "invented" during the Industrial Revolution (18th and 19th centuries CE). She writes, "Language changed from the cosmological and theological to the biological" (DeFranza, page 136). Rather than considering a woman to be a "lesser" man, sex was redefined as two distinct opposites with nothing between them:

> The middle ground had been emptied of the ambiguous cases that once occupied it: hermaphrodites, natural eunuchs, castrated eunuchs, effeminate men, and virile women. Thus, the modern period bequeathed a legacy of two opposite and incommensurable sexes, unified by the belief in the possession of a sexless soul in the Christian tradition or a sexless mind in the tradition of Enlightenment liberalism. (DeFranza, page 136)

In other words, this big shift toward thinking about biology determining sex and gender happened really late (18th and 19th centuries CE).

In her 1995 book, *Making the Difference: Gender, Personhood, and Theology*, Elaine Graham explains that there was a critical paradigm shift between the ancient view that someone's social position determined sex differentiation and the modern view that someone's physical body determines sex differentiation:

> According to ancient, mediaeval and renaissance accounts, physical bodies could experience profound and miraculous transformations. They saw social sex (gender) as foundational, and biological sex as mutable; thus the notion of an 'essential' maleness or femaleness resting in the body was foreign to them. Only when political and scientific changes displaced a

> fixed ordering of social and gender classes did it become expedient to root explanations of the social order in appeals to nature, thus paving the way for a 'two-sex' model which located 'difference' in biology, and rendered sex as primary and bipolar. (Graham, page 127)

In other words, the ancients were not thinking about bodies when they were talking about sex and gender. For them, the body was just one characteristic—and not the most important one.

In her 2003 dissertation, "The Hidden Eunuchs of the Hebrew Bible: Uncovering an Alternate Gender," Janet Everhart highlights developments in the 20th century CE emerging from feminist and gender studies, which specifically differentiate between the categories of "sex" (as biological) and "gender" (as socially constructed). Everhart goes on to argue (following Graham) for a multidimensional, dialectic model of sex and gender:

> Challenges to the distinction between sex and gender were precipitated, in part, by new social and scientific studies that demonstrate the breakdown of many binary oppositions. ... Increasingly, gender theorists agree with Elaine Graham's assessment that neither biological determinism nor social constructionism provides an adequate theoretical model of sex or gender. Graham suggests, as a helpful alternative, a dialectical account of gender that "sees a complex and multidimensioned relationship between biology, social conditioning, and individual consciousness." (Everhart, page 14)

In other words, we are less than one hundred years into this idea that biological sex is seperate from socially constructed gender.

Please note that, in *OtherWise Christian*, I will not be stressing distinctions between "sex" (as biological) and "gender" (as socially constructed). Instead, I will explore the entire constellation of identities and experiences centered around sex and gender, while embracing what I believe to be a healthy level of ambiguity that should allow for the Bible stories (especially those stories of OtherWise-gendered people) to be our priority and focus without imposing too much of a modern framework upon them.

What then of "natural law"? What then of the "obvious"? The irony of the Western conception of gender and the argument from "natural law" is not just that it is a relatively recent invention but that it persists despite all evidence to the contrary:

> In the ancient world, where there was language for eunuchs, hermaphrodites, and androgynes, people were able to see them, laws governed them, and places in society were carved out where they could

> live and contribute to the life of the community. Such is no longer the case. (DeFranza, page 137)

Nonetheless, from biological sciences to medicine to sports, there is growing evidence of complexity and nuance around sex and gender in both human and animal life. God's creation is so much more interesting than the sloppy and simplistic idea of two and only two "opposite" sexes!

Modern medicine has helped us understand more about how our bodies work and all of the many components that are involved in developing sex characteristics, while progress is also being made in understanding brain development as it influences gender. Julia Epstein summarizes:

> The law assumes a precise contrarity between two sexes, whereas medical science has for several centuries understood sex determination to involve a complex and indefinite mechanism that results in a spectrum of human sexual types rather than in a set of mutually exclusive categories. (Epstein, page 101)

The American Medical Association now argues that gender is "incompletely understood as a binary selection" (2017). The American Psychological Association has concluded "that gender is a non-binary construct that allows for a range of gender identities and that a person's gender identity may not align with sex assigned at birth" (2015).

The bottom line is that neither modern science nor careful observation supports a simplistic understanding of two and only two, mutually exclusive genders. Those who have taken the time to study and observe issues related to sex and gender have told us in many different ways that gender and sex are complicated. Arguments that OtherWise-gendered people are "sick," "sinful," or "do not exist" are actually based on biased assumptions about the way someone thinks things are "supposed to be" more than they reflect "natural law" or thoughtful observation of the natural world.

In Pat Conover's 2002 book, *Transgender Good News*, Conover writes eloquently about a more holistic view of natural law and natural theology that includes insights from modern science as well as the all of our lived experiences:

> Good natural theology begins with an appreciation not only of the Creator who has given us the manifest world, but also of the Creator who has given us the opportunity to experience the eternals. We honor the Creator when we celebrate these gifts and use them to guide our participation in giving life and shape to the eternals. Our artistic creations,

> our scientific understanding, our civilizations, our sexual sharing and gender relationships can express the eternals. (Conover, page 209)

If God made everything, then God made our bodies and our brains. God made hormones and chromosomes and brain chemistry that come in all kinds of varieties and combinations. In other words, God made us transgender. God made us intersex. God made us all kinds of different ways. God made us extraordinary. God made us unique. God made us gifted. We, too, are the diversity of God's creation. God saw what God made and God saw that it was good.

♡

You are loved. When they call you impossible. When they call you exceptional. When they cannot hide their surprise. You are loved.

Chapter 5
In the Beginning...?

Look at the new thing
I am going to do.
It is already happening.
Don't you see it?
I will make a road in the desert
and rivers in the dry land.

Isaiah 43:19
New Century Version

As we saw in the last chapter, the idea that sex and gender are binary is a relatively recent development. It has not been the common understanding "from the beginning." Megan DeFranza credits influential theologian, Karl Barth (20th century CE), with pulling together a variety of threads to create a relational model of sex and gender that supports differentiation between men and women as central to the *imago Dei* or "image of God":

> Barth was the first to connect the image of God, not to an extrabodily, sexless, divine substance, but to human being *as* sexually differentiated. For Barth sex/gender differentiation represents the "center of humanity" and is inherently connected to sexuality. ... Even where Barth's proposal has been roundly critiqued, it is impossible to overestimate the significance of his reflections for subsequent theological work. (DeFranza, page 148)

When it comes to gender politics in the church, there are two major camps of Christians who like to argue from creation that "God made two genders." Both the "egalitarian" view and a "complementarian" view are different versions of the "obvious" argument that there are two and only two, mutually exclusive genders, though they will each cite scripture to support their view. The "complementarian" view places women in a subordinate role to men, while the "egalitarian" view makes men and women equal. Many other books have been written around these tensions without even considering transgender, intersex, or other similar experiences. However, both views affirm binary thinking about sex and gender on theological grounds and thus create the lens through which many Christians view transgender identities and experiences.

To put it another way, these views assert that God ordained for there to be two and only two genders from the beginning of creation. Therefore, since God made it that way, humans need to live within that framework (including the gender they were assigned at birth as well as heterosexual marriage). Genesis 1:26–27 and Genesis 2:18–25 as well as "natural law" are often cited as justifications. In a groundbreaking 1997 article in *Theology & Sexuality*, Victoria Kolakowski summarized the approach:

> The physical complementarity of male and female sexual organs, combined with their role in procreation, has led to a dominant view of human sexuality based upon presumption of a 'natural' purpose of sexuality grounded in procreation. ... In this respect many Christians, both Catholics and Protestants, have articulated a 'natural law' understanding of human sexuality. (Kolakowski, "Toward a Christian Ethical Response to Transsexual Persons," page 17)

In *Transforming: The Bible and the Lives of Transgender Christians*, Austen Hartke (drawing on the work of Mark Yarhouse) describes two approaches to transgender identity that draw on these binary assumptions about sex and gender. The first is labeled the "integrity" framework:

> Someone who holds to this framework would consider conflict between one's assigned sex and gender identity sinful because it messes with what they believe to be the strictly male or female nature God gives each of us. ... [P]roponents of this view tend to see any attempt to move away from one's assigned sex as rebellion against what God has ordained. (Hartke, page 34)

Hartke also outlines the "disability" framework (again drawing on Yarhouse), which considers gender dysphoria to be a symptom of original sin. In this approach, being transgender is not a sin in and of itself and transgender people are considered victims or patients (with a mental illness), who should be treated with compassion.

Hartke draws the distinction between these two frameworks as follows:

> This change in moral status is the main difference between the [integrity] framework and the disability framework. In the former, the transgender person is deliberately disobeying God; in the latter, they're merely a victim of original sin like every other human being. This distinction can cause a radical shift in attitude toward trans people, because it means that they can receive compassionate pastoral care that doesn't shame them for their thoughts, feelings, and internal experiences. (Hartke, page 36)

Certainly, thinking of transgender people as broken, sick, or mentally ill is a kindness compared to a worldview that believes transgender people are morally corrupt. Yet, underneath each of these frameworks is that fundamental assumption that transgender people are some kind of wrong. We can see hierarchical thinking persisting through the centuries from Greek and Roman philosophers telling us that transgender people are "less than" other parts of God's creation.

The argument from the "obvious" is a slippery and dangerous one, whether we call it "natural law" or "complementarian theology." In order to maintain the Western worldview on gender, any and all contradictory evidence must be labeled "deviant" or "defective." If there are two and only two genders, then intersex people are a "problem" that needs to be "fixed," and transgender people are either "misguided" victims or "dangerous" rogues. In each case, they must be led or coerced into compliance.

Both the "complementarian" and the "egalitarian" theological views assume that there are two and only two acceptable and God-ordained options for sex/gender (despite all social and scientific evidence to the contrary), though the "egalitarian" view may be more adaptable in terms of integrating other kinds of diversity. As we will see in upcoming chapters, there are many alternate conclusions that can be drawn from reading Christian scripture—conclusions that do not jump to the misguided conclusion that being transgender is inherently wrong.

Meanwhile, trying to force God's good creation to conform to the narrow, modern Western ideology of two and only two, mutually exclusive genders causes immense harm. Intersex activists are increasingly visible in their efforts to confront the stigma, shame, and violence imposed on them by medical professionals (sometimes with the consent of ill-informed parents). Laws are beginning to be passed in some jurisdictions that are intended to prevent "corrective" surgeries on infants and children. Likewise, transgender people (as well as same-gender-loving people) are resisting "therapies" that try to teach or train people to align more closely with the gender they were assigned at birth. Laws are also being passed to outlaw this kind of "reparative therapy" because of the well-documented harm it causes.

The ancient world and the early church were well aware of OtherWise-gendered people, but we, in the modern world, have been bamboozled. Knowledge of gender diversity through the centuries has been suppressed and stolen from us. Much of what now passes for "obvious" in terms of binary sex and gender is really just confirmation bias—that is, the tendency to interpret new evidence as a confirmation of one's existing beliefs or theories.

In order to honor all of God's good creation, we must first open ourselves to the world as it is, not just how we have been taught to see it. We may learn about some things that are new to us! However, gender diversity is actually something very, very old. Some might even say, it has been with us from the beginning.

♡

You are loved. When they try to fit you into their boxes. When they call you deviant or defective. When they call you misguided or dangerous. You are loved.

Chapter 6
Queerly Created in the Image of God

Genesis 1:27

God created the ādām in God's image;
in the image of God [God] created him—
male and female [God] created them.

Genesis 1:27
Translation from *TransTexts*

The mind of God is creative and expansive. Just because other kinds of gender experiences or identities are not mentioned in Genesis 1:27 does not mean that they do not exist. Mentioning "male and female" in the creation accounts neither makes these verses a command nor transforms them into a comprehensive list of gender alternatives. "Male and female" are neither prototype nor ideal forms of gender, any more than "man" is the prototype or ideal form of "woman." In fact, this creation story leaves out all manner of created features, from rivers and marshes to asteroids and planets, from amphibians and arthropods to dusk and dawn. As Megan DeFranza points out,

> Few would argue that these "others" or "hybrids" are a result of the Fall, or that they stray from God's creational intent. Genesis simply does not give us a comprehensive list of all the good things God has made. It is the beginning of the story, painting in broad brush strokes, with so much more to come. (DeFranza, page 177)

In his influential book, *Trans-Gendered: Theology, Ministry, and Communities of Faith*, which was originally published in 2003 and revised in 2018, Justin Tanis notes (citing Nahum M. Sarna),

> The earth-being (*ādām*) created originally is both male and female, created in the image of God. This view is strongly supported by the Hebrew text, which uses the term *ādām*, not as a name as is currently familiar in English, but in description of this being created from the earth. The word *ādām* is a play on the Hebrew word for earth, *'adamah*. Rather than translating this word as a proper name, a more accurate rendering of the word would be "earthling" or "earth-being." Originally, this earthling was one, without

> gender differentiation, encompassing both female and male. (Tanis, page 58)

Throughout the creation accounts, the phrase is *hā-ādām.* The extra "hā" means "the," so it is not Adam, but rather "the *ādām*," not just *an* earth-creature but *the* earth creature.

Because it is a Hebrew and Jewish text, it is important to consult our Jewish siblings for more context about this verse from Genesis. In 2008, Rabbis Reuben Zellman and Elliot Kukla created a ground-breaking online resource called *TransTexts* which has since been relocated to the Keshet website. It turns out that rabbis and Jewish scholars have been discussing Genesis 1:27 for centuries! Many of the questions raised have been about the odd use of pronouns and singular/plural, as well as discrepancies in comparison with the Genesis 2 creation story.

TransTexts articulates the grammar question:

> An examination of the entire verse reveals that the first created human is referred to first in the singular, and then promptly in the plural. This leads to the questions: Was that first human a single or a multiple being? How can this discrepancy be explained, and what might it have to do with the "male and female" reference in the same verse? (TransTexts, "Queerly Created," "What problem were the rabbis trying to solve?")

In her 2009 contribution to *Torah Queeries: Weekly Commentaries on the Hebrew Bible*, Rabbi Margaret Moers Wenig promoted the idea that this verse is an example of a "merism" (Wenig, page 16). In other words, it is an example of a figure of speech where the whole is represented by listing only two of its components. Another example occurs in Psalm 139 when the psalmist indicates that God knows "when I sit down and when I rise up" as a way of saying that God knows every action (not just the specific instances of changing positions). Likewise, when we talk about God as the Alpha and Omega, we are pointing not only to the beginning and the end, but also between and beyond. We are pointing to all that lies between those endpoints, as well as everything beyond them. We say Alpha and Omega, beginning and end, but we mean all that ever was or will be. Similarly, Wenig suggests that this verse means God brought every bit of every gender into existence (not just the specific instances of male and female).

According to *TransTexts*, Rabbi Yirmiyah ben Elazar, Rabbi Shmuel Bar Nachman, and Rabbi Tanchuma all discussed the nature of the first human being in *Genesis Rabbah 8:1* (circa 400 CE). Each rabbi concluded that the first human being was either bigendered or genderless. Rabbi Yirmiyah ben Elazar said the *ādām* was an *androginos* (wholly male and wholly female, both). Rabbi Shmuel Bar Nachman argued that the *ādām* was half male and half female. Rabbi Tanchuma argued that the *ādām* was a *golem*, "a formless and infinite mass. Such a creature would have neither a discernable sex, nor even a defined physical form" (*TransTexts*, "Queerly Created," "Commentary").

Virginia Mollenkott gave us the first book-length treatment of transgender and intersex theological concerns with her 2001 *Omnigender: A Trans-Religious Approach*, which was updated in 2007. Mollenkott cites influential Hebrew scholar Phyllis Trible as arguing that the first human being was sexually undifferentiated, "one creature who was... neither male or female or a combination of both" (Mollenkott, 2007 edition, page 99). Mollenkott goes on to provocatively call this first human being a "gender outlaw" (Mollenkott, 2007 edition, page 99):

> According to this very ancient interpretation, binary gender would be a later development, not the first intention of the Creator but provided subsequently for the sake of human companionship. From this angle, hermaphrodites or intersexuals could be viewed as reminders of Original Perfection. (Mollenkott, 2007 edition, page 99)

If the *ādām* is made in the image of God, what does this also tell us about the nature of God? That God is *both* male and female? An *androginos*, fully male and fully female? A genderless *golem*? It is not a stretch to argue that God is intersex or non-binary, between or beyond what we think of as male or female.

Tanis works around some questions related to the gender of God, concluding,

> Yet an intersexed or transgendered image of God, one that embodies both male and female, is more biblically accurate than one that forces God into a single-gendered box. ... People who speak of God as fully and wholly male ignore those parts of sacred texts that refer to God in feminine terms. The intersexed nature of God is thus hidden from [the] view of worshippers and believers as certainly as we conceal the evidence of intersexed and transgendered humans. The time has come to tell the truth about God even as we tell our own truths. (Tanis, page 137–138)

Theologians such as Trible and Mollenkott would be quick to warn that all God-language is metaphorical. As Mollenkott puts it,

> [W]e cannot argue... that God is literally androgynous or intersexual, any more than we can depict God as literally male or literally female. But neither can anyone claim... that our current male-female polarization is based on the image of God. It isn't. (Mollenkott, 2007 edition, page 100)

Joy Ladin takes this question about the nature of God in a different direction in her book, *The Soul of the Stranger: Reading God and Torah from a Transgender Perspective* (2019):

> [T]he God I saw in the Torah seemed basically the same as the God I knew in my life: invisible, bodiless, everywhere and nowhere, alive and present but not in ways that made sense in human terms. One minute, God is creating the world, the next, God is destroying it with a flood. On this page, God promises Sarah and Abraham a son; a few pages later, God tells Abraham to kill that son. That was the God I knew—a loving, dangerous, incomprehensible God who kept me from killing myself one night and woke me the next morning to a life I couldn't bear to live. I made no sense in terms of binary gender; God made no sense in human terms at all. (Ladin, *The Soul of the Stranger,* page 63)

Ultimately, it is not for us to understand, label, or categorize God. Afterall, God calls themself, "I am who I am" or "I will be what I will be" (Exodus 3:14). This is a God who transcends labels and categories—and we are made in the image of that binary-busting God! We will consider related insights from Ladin in chapter 21. Rather than emphasizing words and labels, this God is best known through relationship with each of us.

Austen Hartke also delves into the *imago dei* (in conversation with M Barclay) and concludes,

> So how is God's image manifested in our bodies? In the same way that it's manifested in the rest of our being. The image of God was not given to humankind in bits and pieces, with some living in your left arm and another bit in your soul and another bit in your ability to argue and reason. It is a gift that resonates throughout all that we are, like the deep tones of a bell rung far away. It awakens us and moves us forward toward God and toward each other. (Hartke, page 58)

And so we are connected, each of us, to God—and to one another through God. Our gender (male, female, or OtherWise) is just one of the many ways that we relate one to another, with each and every earth creature embodying some spark of the divine image.

♡

You are loved. When you cannot figure it out. When you cannot be figured out. When you feel connected. When you feel disconnected. You are loved.

Chapter 7
The Earth Creature(s)

Genesis 2:18–25

And the LORD God said,
It is not good
that the [ādām] *should be alone;*
I will make him an help meet for him.

Genesis 2:18 KJV

...and the LORD God built
that which he had taken
from the side of the [ādām]
into a woman
and brought her unto the [ādām].

Genesis 2:22
Jubilee Bible 2000 Version
With transliteration added

The other creation story (Genesis 2) also appears to invoke gender. Obviously, this story is in dialogue with the Genesis 1 text within both Jewish and Christian traditions. Throughout this second version of the creation story, we are told again about the creation of the *ādām*, the first earth creature, even though most English translations make it "the man." Congruent with ideas offered in the previous chapter, this being is not a human male. All we know is that the *ādām* is the first human being created by God.

In this story, we learn that the earth creature (*ādām*) is lonely and that this is the reason that God goes on to create animals and eventually a second human being. God creates a help meet for the first earth creature. Justin Tanis points out that,

> The word used for "helper" here, *'ēzer*, is used most commonly to refer to God's assistance to humanity and implies a superior help. The point of this passage is not to set up a hierarchy of humanity but rather to show and correct the problem of loneliness. ... Our reading of this passage can

> conclude, then, that gender is not the problem, but our isolation from love, connection, and relationship. (Tanis, pages 61–62)

After God tries to match the first earth creature up with a variety of animals to cure the first earth creature's loneliness, God finally creates a suitable helper—a partner, a lifesaver, or perhaps a deliverer.

While many translations interpret the word *tsela* as "rib," it is more appropriately translated as "side," as in the side of a tent or building. There is nowhere else in scripture where this word is translated as "rib." Meanwhile, understanding that this partner/deliverer earth creature was created from the side the first earth creature fits nicely with arguments about the first creation story that suggested the original *ādām* may have been half male and half female, both male and female, or lacking sexual differentiation.

Other interpretations of this word *tsela* include the idea that God may have taken an extra appendage or a literal extra rib from the side of the first earth creature. Regardless of whether the second earth creature was created from a side or a rib or an unspecified appendage, Liam Hooper points out that this "sacred surgery" changed the first earth creature. While the original earth creature was presumably a wholly self-sustaining being, made in the image of a self-sufficient God, the two post-operative earth beings that emerge from that first surgery need one another. Indeed, the first earth creature's being alone was the only part of creation that was labeled "not good."

Those who advocate for a "complementarian" reading of this text are correct in finding an emphasis on relationship. However, the "complementarian" argument reads a lot into these turns of phrase when it suggests that sexuality is what saves us from loneliness and isolation and brings us into deeper connection (making Adam and Eve the prototype for such sexualized community). Megan DeFranza challenges this move as problematic (DeFranza, pages 218–221), noting that no individual (since the first earth creature!) has actually been born into isolation. Rather, we are all born into communities of interdependence long before our sexuality emerges.

DeFranza further counters that "Envisioning sexuality as that which enables bonding is not a remedy for a society that knows much of sexuality and very little of bonded faithful relationships of any stripe" (DeFranza, page 220). She goes on, "Marital love is distorted and diminished when it is viewed primarily through the lens of the sexual" (DeFranza, page 224). Instead, DeFranza argues that Adam and Eve can be viewed and reclaimed as the "progenitors of human relationality" (DeFranza, page 238) without falling for these overly sexualized distortions. DeFranza suggests that familial relations, as exemplified by the love shared between siblings or in families built through adoption, are more Biblical analogies for faithful Christian community and the love into which God calls us—not because the analogy to marriage and sexuality is inherently bad (it has its merits), but because emphasizing marriage leads to over-emphasizing the conjugal act to the detriment of all of the other ways that families live together in faithful community.

In the end, this passage seems to have very little to do with gender at all—and everything to do with our connections to one another. As Tanis summed it up,

> This passage reveals to us that God is more concerned with our loneliness than with our gender and longs for us to have an appropriate companion and helper. Love brings completion, not gender, because a man and a woman who are together without love surely do not correct the problem that God identifies in this section. Rather, people who are appropriate companions and helpers for one another bring the creation back to a sense of goodness and completion. (Tanis, page 62)

Joy Ladin draws an even more inclusive conclusion, arguing that, in this text, gender is not created by God at all, but that gender is a human invention that comes later:

> Adam is human before he is gendered; his humanity does not depend on him fitting into a binary gender system, on being a man as opposed to a woman. The Torah presents gender not as a built-in aspect of humanity decreed by God, but as a human creation, born out of Adam's response to Eve. ... Above all, Genesis lays the ground for accepting people who don't fit binary gender categories by reminding us that people don't have to be gendered to be human. (Ladin, *The Soul of the Stranger*, pages 31–32)

May we all be freed to be the humans that God meant for us to be. May we be empowered to join together as the family of God, siblings in Christ, connected and communing with one another. May we embody the love of God to one another as help meets, partners, lifesavers, and deliverers.

♡

You are loved. When you are with your family. When you are in community. When you are lonely or alone. You are loved.

SECTION THREE
Clobber Verses

Chapter 8
Biblical Self-Defense

Be strong and courageous.
Do not be afraid or terrified
because of them,
for the LORD your God
goes with you;
he will never leave you
nor forsake you.

Deuteronomy 31:6 NIV

Because discussions around Christianity and sexuality for many years revolved around six to ten "clobber verses," an assumption is often made that the Bible speaks similarly about transgender experiences. In fact, there are really only two "clobber verses" that deserve serious consideration in regard to transgender experiences. I will review those in the next two chapters.

Unfortunately, many people remain confused about what it means to be transgender and how it does (or does not) relate to sexual orientation. Simply put, gender identity is about who you are, and sexual orientation is about whom you prefer to have romantic or sexual relations with. So, if a Bible verse talks about who lies down with whom, that is about sexuality and perhaps sexual orientation, not gender identity.

Many books and other resources have been written to defend against the sexual orientation "clobber verses." I will not be rehearsing them, but I will list some trusted resources in appendix A for your consideration. It is important to acknowledge that those verses still get used haphazardly against people of transgender experience! This is another example of assaults from people who speak with "authority" without bothering to seek understanding of either sacred people or sacred text. Cultural assumptions, too often, take precedence over "what the Bible (actually) says."

Justin Tanis summarizes the dynamic in this way,

> When transgendered people hear words of condemnation, rather than simply "taking it," we can take the Bible and talk back. The Bible should never serve as a weapon. Nor should it be taken away from us as a tool for spiritual growth and understanding. Certain passages speak directly to our experiences as gender-variant people and these verses should serve as

> a resource for people for whom the Bible has spiritual meaning and authority. Do not let people who preach condemnation take that tool away from you. (Tanis, page 84)

Equipping you to take the Bible back from trans-antagonistic Christians is one of the tasks of *OtherWise Christian.* However, it is not the only task—or even the most important one. In the end, your well-being is of the utmost importance, and doing battle with Bible bashers can have deep and enduring impacts.

Engaging with trans-antagonistic Christians can be especially challenging if they are hurling cultural assumptions rather than having a thoughtful discussion about text or tradition. In some cases, it may be useful to invite the trans-antagonist to get more specific about where their sense of judgment and condemnation is coming from. However, safer spirituality means that you also need to be ready to protect yourself from what may come forth in that process. Often, those that use religious authority (whether the Bible, religious credentials, or other) to shut down a conversation or wage war have a hidden (or not so hidden) agenda around propping up their own sense of superiority.

Give yourself permission to step away from conversations that are causing harm. Allow yourself to let go of encounters that are based on thoughtless assumptions. Watch out for people who are more worried about being "right" than in supporting your liberation. Keep your toolkit of affirmations close at hand to help you remind yourself of the extraordinary gift that is you. Forgive yourself, if you're unable to counter centuries of entrenched colonization with a quick rebuttal every time.

Are you dealing with a cultural Christian who is parroting what they have heard from some other authority figure? Are you dealing with someone who has actually examined the Bible thoughtfully? Are there assumptions being made about who has more expertise or authority when it comes to the Bible and gender in the ancient world? What other kinds of assumptions are being made about gender and Christianity and who controls the conversation?

Near the end of their book, Pat Conover acknowledges the power dynamics involved in theological conversation:

> Some writers do theology as if they had a privileged grounding for declaring spiritual truth to others. As one who has experienced the love of God, I too feel that I have something precious to share. But I am aware that my personal sharing is testimony for the reader to evaluate rather than a privileged grounding for declaration. (Conover, page 204)

We can agree or disagree on any point of theological concern, but your testimony about God's working in your life is your own. Your conscience, your moral compass, your theological imagination is yours and yours alone. These are precious gifts. Any spiritual authority who requires you to give up your own wrestling with God in favor of their somehow superior authority is one you would do well to be suspicious of.

Conover goes on to acknowledge that "Christendom has hurt so many transgender people so badly" (Conover, page 205). Conover models the kind of humility and grace that one must look for in anyone who claims to speak of the Christian faith:

> Even though I write as a transgender person, I join the confession of aware Christians that we share in the sin and alienation done in our common name. We can do better. (Conover, page 205)

Learning about gender diversity in the Christian Bible is not a quick fix for the realities of transphobia and trans-antagonism widely found in Christian culture, or for the ways that these perspectives align themselves with settler-colonial values (including white supremacy and Christian supremacy), which obsess about being "right." However, familiarizing yourself with "what the Bible says" about gender diversity should help you distinguish between toxic cultural influences and biblical misappropriation.

♡

You are loved. When they think they are better than you. When they are stubborn and will not be reasonable. When they want to cause you harm. You are loved.

Chapter 9
Cross-dressing and Drag

Deuteronomy 22:5

A woman should not put on the apparel of a man;
nor should a man wear the clothing of a woman—
for whoever does these things—
it is a to'evah [completely off-limits behavior]
to the Eternal your God.

Deuteronomy 22:5
TransTexts translation

"Law and order" kinds of Christians may pick and choose (in other words, cherry-pick or proof-text) particular verses to be used as a weapon to condemn or judge. Deuteronomy (and Leviticus) are great sources for such one-liners, including the anti-gay favorite "Thou shalt not lie with mankind, as with womankind: it is abomination [*to'evah*]" (Leviticus 18:22 KJV). In my experience, this English word, "abomination," has become almost synonymous with Christians spitting hatred at same-gender-loving people.

TransTexts clarifies what is lost in translation from the original Hebrew text when it was brought into English:

> The Hebrew word "*to'evah*" is most commonly translated into English as "abomination." However, "abomination" has moral overtones that do not fully capture the Hebrew. Although this term is used to refer to forbidden sexual practices, in the book of Deuteronomy it is also used to refer to animals that are forbidden for consumption (see Chapter 14) such as deer, goat and antelope. This demonstrates that unlike the English word "abomination" the Hebrew "*to'evah*" is morally neutral. A better translation might be "completely off-limits." (*TransTexts*, "Crossdressing and Drag," "Glossary")

In other words, a literal reading of this verse from the Hebrew makes cross-dressing forbidden, but not a disgraceful monstrosity to God.

Nonetheless, Deuteronomy 22:5 is a major "clobber passage" for people of transgender experience. It is often read to mean that everyone should always adorn themself as is typical for one's *assigned* gender.

However, that is not actually what the verse says! It does not in any way define man or woman as referring to *assigned* gender. So the same verse can also be read to mean that everyone should always adorn themself as is typical for one's *affirmed* gender. Once we affirm that someone's *true* gender may not be congruent with their *assigned* gender, this verse compels us to embody that *true* self more fully and openly. In any case, it is clear that cross-dressing was common enough in the ancient world that the scribes and lawmakers were concerned about it for some reason. If people were abiding by the two-and-only-two-mutually-exclusive-genders mode in the ancient world, then there would have been no need for this prohibition at all.

A common liberal retort disregards one-liners from Deuteronomy out of hand. Virginia Mollenkott offers one popular liberal argument, based on the understanding that these prohibitions are a part of Israel's Holiness Codes, which were designed to create distinctions between the Jewish people and competing Pagan practices of the time. They served a purpose to preserve and protect the unique character of the Jewish people:

> It made sense for ancient Israel to draw boundaries between its own customs and beliefs and those of surrounding cultures. And it made sense for the Apostle Paul to draw boundaries between a nascent struggling Christianity and the religions that surrounded it. But in our society, both Judaism and Christianity are so well established that they need no self-protective definition. And people who are truly full of faith in God have no need to fear people who differ from themselves. (Mollenkott, 2007 edition, page 107–108)

Pat Conover continues their examination of the text by looking to Jesus and how he handled purity laws in the Torah:

> In the time of Jesus, the Pharisees, Sadducees, and Essenes were taking paths that emphasized the cultural distinctness in the midst of the Roman Empire. Jesus, in sharp distinction, challenged the cultural laws of Judaism that had no saving power. Jesus continuously placed himself in opposition to the distractions of the purity laws. (Conover, page 221)

In Christian worship settings, people will say that Jesus Christ made the "Old Law" irrelevant for those who are a part of the "New Covenant." Christians often claim that "freedom in Christ" means Christians are not bound by the Mosaic Law, because such things have been washed away with our sins.

Justin Tanis sums up his assessment of several discussion points with this comment,

> Note, however, that modern Christianity, and many in modern Judaism, no longer literally follow the prohibitions listed in Deuteronomy. ... For me, the most compelling argument against this passage as a prohibition against cross-dressing is that we fail to follow any of the other directives around it. (Tanis, pages 65–66)

Unfortunately, these methods for dismissing the Deuteronomy 22:5 clobber text lean toward the idea that the Jewish text is outdated and/or that Jewish tradition is oppressive. Even in the words I have chosen to write or quote above, we see words such as "irrelevant" and "distraction" used to characterize Jewish tradition, along with the suggestion that Jesus "challenged" Judaism and brought "freedom." At every turn, Judaism is characterized as a problem to be solved, even though Jesus was Jewish for his entire life.

This Christian theological approach, called "supersessionism" or "replacement theology" is a specifically Christian sort of theological anti-Semitism, which sees Christianity as not just an alternate path out of ancient Judaism, but as specifically replacing both Judaism and the Jewish people. Since Christian supremacy is so closely connected to both white supremacy and the Western gender narrative, it is important that we grapple with whether a dismissive approach to the Hebrew text really moves us toward broad-based transgender liberation. Even in its most benign expression, supersessionism supports the idea that sacred Jewish text and tradition are outdated or archaic.

At the very least, this move drives a wedge between transgender Christians and transgender Jews who we might hope would be working together. At the worst, it deeply warps our perception of the religious tradition that is the closest cousin of Christianity and prevents us from learning from the wisdom of those who have, collectively, taken the Hebrew text most seriously over many centuries and generations. Rather than learning from and being in solidarity with our Jewish siblings who are working on similar issues right now, Christians, too often, settle for inaccurate stereotypes and caricatures, while ignoring 2,000 years of Jewish scholarship and debate. Judaism is a living, breathing tradition, and we are better for it when we have the wisdom to explore the vibrant resources they have to offer.

When reading the Hebrew sections of the Christian Bible, and especially Deuteronomy (and Leviticus), it can be useful to examine how Jewish scholars and religious leaders have used the text. Another section of *TransTexts* provides a summary of some of those views:

> All of the mitzvot that are nestled around our verse point to a world of compassion, where we are careful not to damage relations between beings. This biblical context was doubtlessly known by our commentators when

> they interpreted this verse. All of the primary early commentators on this verse offer non-literal interpretations. Their readings of the text all reflect the verse's context: embedded amongst ethical mitzvot. In the Talmud this verse prohibits transgressing someone else's space. According to Rashi this verse prohibits sexual betrayal, while for Rambam this verse prohibits idolatry. All of these readings understand the prohibition to be not about cross-dressing per se, but about damaging relationships between us, our neighbors, loved ones or God. (*TransTexts*, "Crossdressing and Drag," "What is the context of this passage?")

In other words, several Jewish scholars have argued that Deuteronomy 22:5 should not be taken literally—that cross-dressing itself is not as important as the intention and context for cross-dressing. Using Purim traditions as an example, one discussion revolves around a positive exception for when cross-dressing is simpy intended to bring joy and happiness. Some scholars have also pointed out that gender norms for clothing are not absolute but, rather, are defined by the local community. For further details, please review the "Crossdressing and Drag" section of *TransTexts* where you will find a plethora of relevant information and beautiful, nuanced interpretation from within a Jewish context.

Certainly, ethical conversations can be had about how we might best adorn ourselves to the glory of God within a particular cultural context, but Christians too often reduce the Mosaic law to a simple book of rules to be used to include or exclude, praise or condemn. A more Jewish consideration of the Hebrew text indicates that there are multiple non-literal interpretations among the rabbis of old, who were much closer to the historical context in which the verse was written. Furthermore, many of these readings bring us back to ethical conversations about how we ought to treat one another (rather than using sacred text to clobber and condemn one another). In short, following the wisdom of our Jewish ancestors, we can be confident that the Jewish tradition represented in Deuteronomy 22:5 is much more concerned with how we treat one another, with our being honest and forthright about our true identities, and with honoring God, than it is concerned about what we wear from day to day.

♡

You are loved. When they make you the problem. When they call you an abomination. When their disgust shows through. You are loved.

Chapter 10
Crushed Testicles and Transgender Women

Deuteronomy 23:1

No man whose testicles have been crushed
or whose penis has been cut off
may enter the LORD's assembly.

Deuteronomy 23:1
Christian Standard Bible

Deuteronomy 23:1 is the other "clobber passage" that people especially like to use against people of transgender experience (and especially transgender women). Leviticus 21:16–21 can be used in a similar way. Certainly, some people weaponize this verse against gender confirmation surgery for transgender women, but not only that. Some will also stretch this verse to imply that anyone considering medical transition or other physical modification is in the wrong—even though they do not make the same argument against medically necessary amputations, breast reconstruction after a mastectomy, tatoos, piercings, or various cosmetic surgeries available in the modern world.

A literal interpretation of this verse would suggest that (post-operative) transgender women might need to be expelled from religious congregations (Jewish and Christian) along with men who have undergone vasectomies, men who have had certain cancer treatments, and men who have been injured in the pelvic/pubic region (for instance, in military combat or a car accident). Such a conclusion would align comfortably with the male-dominated Western gender narrative that privileges and prioritizes men and male bodies that are endowed with certain physical features. It might also make sense in the ancient Greek or Roman worldview, which privileged manly men over effeminate men, eunuchs, and other "misbegotten" beings (see chapter 4).

Those referred to in Deuteronomy 23:1 generally would have been referred to as eunuchs in the ancient world. We will consider the role of eunuchs extensively as a key biblical example of OtherWise-gendered people in the next section. For now, I will just note that eunuchs without a penis or testicles would not have been considered men in any traditional sense of that sex/gender. They were not considered women, either. According to Megan DeFranza, "While a barren woman remained a woman and an androgyne could be classified as a man, 'eunuch' remained a term of 'in-between-ness'" (DeFranza, page 103).

As discussed in the previous chapter, it would be convenient for Christians to disregard Deuteronomy as wholly irrelevant and move along to other parts of scripture. There is much with which to be uncomfortable in this section. For instance, consistency would demand that children born out of wedlock should also be excluded from congregational life (Deuteronomy 23:2), along with certain "foreign" nationalities (Deuteronomy 23:3–4). However, in moving so quickly and dismissively, we would again miss the rich resource that is the whole of Jewish and Christian scripture in terms of resisting the Western gender narrative. Let us look again to our Jewish siblings.

Noach Dzmura's *Balancing on the Mechitza: Transgender in the Jewish Community* is a ground-breaking collection of reflections by transgender Jews, published in 2010. "The God Thing" is Joy Ladin's contribution to that effort. In it, she reflects,

> Jewish law, even in its most Orthodox forms, is evolving, not static; it takes account of post-Bronze Age advances in medicine and psychology. Non-Orthodox Jewish movements have already moved towards acceptance of transsexuals, and individual rabbis have begun adapting Jewish life-cycle rituals to transsexual transition. (Ladin, *Balancing on the Mechitza*, page 71)

The Committee on Jewish Law and Standards sets *halakhic* (such as keeping kosher, etc.) policy for Rabbinical Assembly rabbis and for the Conservative movement as a whole. This excerpt is from their 2017 document, "Transgender Jews and Halakhah":

> In addressing the questions that arise regarding transgender people in Jewish life, we must keep in mind that although *halakhah* deals with categories, rabbis and halakhists deal with people, and that the transgender community is a large and diverse group of people. ... In order to apply those halakhic categories in ways that are sensitive and compassionate, and at the same time maintain halakhic integrity, we must acknowledge that our understanding of human sex, sexuality, and gender, limited though it may be, is advanced far beyond anything our ancestors could have imagined. The challenge we face is that although *halakhah* is binary in terms of gender, people are not. The Rabbis understood this. They recognized several types of people who did not fit the male/female

> binary. ("Transgender Jews and Halakhah" by Rabbi Leonard A. Sharzer, MD)

The Reform Movement and the Reconstructionist Rabbinical Association, two other contemporary Jewish movements, have made similarly supportive statements.

In Dzmura's introduction to chapter 3 of *Balancing on the Mechitza*, he writes,

> Gender variance is also surprisingly well represented in postbiblical Jewish texts. While Jewish legal texts specify a rigid two-gender grid, the discourse surrounding the law allows for a surprising amount of human variation. (Dzmura, page 158)

In her "Judaism and Gender Issues" contribution to *Balancing on the Mechitza*, Beth Orens describes the position of Orthodox Rabbi Yehuda Waldenberg (also known as, Tzitz Eliezer, 20th and 21st century) who was well-known for his work on issues of medical ethics. Orens quotes Waldenberg on the marital status of "women who changed into men" (Orens, page 226). In other words, he is speaking to the question, "How does gender transition impact the status of a pre-transition (heterosexual) marriage?":

> Because this woman has many signs of being a man which are apparent to the visual sense, she does not require a writ of divorce, because she is truly a man. (Waldenberg as cited by Orens, page 226)

According to Waldenberg, the gender transition simply dissolves the marriage. Orens summarizes further, showing that Waldenberg was equally concerned with men who change into women:

> The source continues to say that in the morning blessings, where a man says, "Blessed are you, Lord our God, King of the Universe, who has not made me a woman," such a man should end the blessing instead, "who has changed me into a man" (Rabbi Waldenberg states elsewhere that a male who becomes female would say "who has changed me according to his will," rather than the standard "who has made me according to his will," which is said by women). (Orens, page 226)

Unfortunately, Rabbi Waldenberg's thoughtful acceptance of transgender identity stands out as a minority among Orthodox Jewish *poskim*. Nonetheless, it is maintained as a viable minority position in the corpus of responsa on halakhic (Jewish legal) issues.

It turns out that Jews have a much more nuanced understanding of the purpose, shape, and interpretation of Jewish law than most Christians do. That should not be surprising. Many modern Jewish leaders have declined to use Deuteronomy 23:1 to condemn transgender women. If the Jewish leaders of our day are not consistently using Deuteronomy 23:1 to take aim at OtherWise-gendered people such as eunuchs and transgender women, then it certainly makes Christians who do so look ignorant and abusive.

Do better, Christians.

♡

You are loved. When you are changing. When they got sticks and stones. When the haters gonna hate. You are loved.

SECTION FOUR
Eunuchs, Eunuchs, and More Eunuchs

Chapter 11
Of Words and Their Many Meanings

May the words of my mouth
and the meditations of my heart
be acceptable in your sight,
Lord, my rock
and my Redeemer.

Psalm 19:14
International Standard Version

Meanings Change

When I started exploring my gender identity in 1998, we were saying "transgendered" (among other things), but somewhere around 2006 "best practices" evolved and that particular word went out of style. When I was pulling references for this book, I ran across an online review of a ground-breaking book published in 2002 by a transgender author that had used "transgendered" as a part of the book's title. The online reviewer quipped,

> Transgendered is not a word. Using this word in just the title already shows ignorance and a lack of wanting to understand trans people. Not to mention it's grammatically incorrect as well. (2016 online review of a book that was published in 2002)

The irony is that the reviewer is not entirely wrong. "Transgendered" is no longer considered grammatically correct nor a "best practice." However, the reviewer was definitely missing the critical context that this book was published before that consensus had been formed. The book's author was by no means ignorant! They were simply writing in an earlier era.

A lot happened in that 14 years between the 2002 book and the 2016 book review. "Best practices" around language for transgender communities have been changing rapidly since the 1990s when the rise of internet communication exponentially increased our capacity to be connected and in conversation with one another. Imagine how meanings may have shifted over centuries on top of translation from languages such as Hebrew, Greek, and Aramaic or between various cultural and religious worldviews!

Reflecting on what she dubs "word-elimination" and "word-sabotage" strategies used by activists to discount particular language as oppressive, Julia Serano argues that these well-meaning modern campaigns to discredit particular words can actually cause harm. I agree with Serano that dismissing another person's word choice out of hand is problematic, even as I respect efforts to develop coherent "best practices." In *OtherWise Christian*, you will find a variety of quotes using terms that are no longer in fashion. Rather than try to avoid or alter such references, I have quoted them as written by the original author (with an occasional warning if I am aware that an outdated term is now considered a slur).

FORGE published a helpful resource in 2012 called the "Terms Paradox," which puts some of these language complexities into perspective. The first half of the paradox says, "Terms are crucial. Finding out what terms a person uses and then using their language is a primary way of conveying respect and openness." The second half of the paradox says, "Terms are meaningless. Terms tell you almost none of what you need to know to... have respectful, meaningful interactions."

Communication is dependent on having some shared vocabulary, even as meanings shift and evolve over time. On the one hand, we do need to encourage respectful and culturally competent language. However, it is also important that we not let the impulse to standardize language distract us from honoring the unique experiences and expressions of real-life OtherWise-gendered people. It is especially important when we engage with people across cultural differences that we not colonize their experiences with our own Western understandings and priorities. When we do, we not only cause harm to the relationship, but we also fail to benefit from the wisdom of other cultural contexts that have so much to teach us.

Eunuchs

These kinds of tensions and evolutions in language are important to keep in mind as we look back over a lively 2,000+ years of conversation in several languages about an identity word like "eunuch." Not only has the term "eunuch" functioned over many centuries and cultures, but it is mentioned in the Christian Bible at least 50 times. The Hebrew word is transliterated *saris*, which, according to Strong's lexicon, appears 42 times in the Hebrew text (in 10 different books, from Genesis to Daniel). The comparable Greek word is *eunouchos*, which according to Strong's lexicon, appears eight times (all in Matthew and Acts).

If the world is divided into two and only two mutually exclusive genders, then eunuchs were something else entirely. According to Megan DeFranza, "Much like the term 'intersex,' 'eunuch' was an umbrella concept—a word to cover a range of phenomena wherein humans did not measure up to the male ideal" (DeFranza, page 68). DeFranza spends an entire chapter unpacking this range of physical traits, roles, and expectations in Greek, Roman, Jewish, and Christian contexts through the centuries.

DeFranza describes "eunuchs of the sun" (*saris khama*). "Babies born with ambiguous or poorly formed genitals were considered eunuchs from the day of their birth" (DeFranza, page 71). Yet, this is not the only category with which intersex people might have been identified, since not all intersex people have ambiguous genitals. Other intersex conditions might result in identities such as barren women, hermaphrodites, or androgynes. So, there is no direct equivalence between the identity of eunuch in the ancient world and the identity of intersex that we know now, although there is likely some significant overlap.

Another type of eunuch is someone who was born with a typical male body but who was castrated, either before or after puberty. According to DeFranza,

> In the Roman era, ritual castration was a part of the cult of Cybele, which was derived from prehistoric fertility religions, worship of the *Magna Mater* (Great Mother), and was integrated into the Roman pantheon as the *Mater Deum* (Mother of the Gods). These castrated priests were known in the ancient world as the *galli*. (DeFranza, page 77)

Some of the tension in Jewish and Christian traditions regarding eunuchs very likely stems from their role in other religious traditions. According to DeFranza,

> From the ancient Hebrew perspective, castrated eunuchs were quintessential foreigners, the epitome of "other." Castration was forbidden within Judaism... It is probably their association with ancient fertility religions that stands behind their exclusion from the assembly of the Lord in Deuteronomy 23:1. (DeFranza, page 78)

In addition to religious significance, castration has physical implications. Castrated eunuchs would clearly be understood as "less than" men (see chapter 4), as the removal of testes (and related decline in testosterone) would have had a feminizing effect. DeFranza notes, "Boys who were castrated before puberty developed unique physical characteristics, distinct from men and women" (DeFranza, page 79). Sean D. Burke provides specific details:

> Some of these characteristics were not specifically gendered... Other characteristics, however, were gendered as specifically feminine: eunuchs castrated before puberty lacked the facial and body hair characteristic of adult males; they had wider hips and higher voices than adult males; they tended to have less-developed musculature than adult males; and they tended to have some enlargement of the breasts and buttocks due to a distribution of body fat that was more characteristic of adult females. In addition their penises remained small and immature. (Burke, pages 108–109)

DeFranza points out, "In the Talmud, eunuchs are derided for unmanly characteristics" (DeFranza, page 79).

The physical implications of castration were not just a matter of outward appearance. Castration also disrupted the eunuch's fertility, which in turn proscribed the individual's place within community life. Austen Hartke points out,

> In ancient Israelite society, children were not only a blessing from God; they were also your legacy. Offspring assured that you would be remembered and guaranteed a future for the community. ... The ability to produce offspring was such an intrinsic part of Israelite identity that it seemed nonnegotiable. When eunuchs experienced the physical cutting off that changed their identity, they also experienced a cutting off from the future and from their culture. (Hartke, pages 95–96)

Nonetheless, the origin of the term "eunuch" in Greek points to roles and duties, not to a physical form or feature. DeFranza explains,

> The Greek term *eunoukhous* is... literally 'the one holding/guarding/keeping watch over the bed,' typically the bedchamber of the king... The corresponding Hebrew term is *saris*, from *sar* in Babylonian (an older Semitic language), which means 'king.' *Saris* is translated 'eunuch 'or 'official' depending on the context. (DeFranza, page 73, citing Ringrose and Scholz)

The role of the eunuch in royal courts is well documented across several cultures and centuries in the ancient world, despite the scorn frequently expressed toward castration. According to DeFranza,

> Eunuchs handled everything from powerful administrative functions and military command to cup-bearing and guarding the intimate spaces of their masters and mistresses. Cut off from their families of origin, raised to see the family of their master as their own family, and prevented from fathering children of their own, eunuchs owed their entire identity, complete loyalty, to their masters. Their inability to procreate barred them

> from claiming power in their own name, and also from producing heirs who might challenge the dynastic authority of the sacred king or emperor. Their gender ambiguity also enabled them to mediate between men and women, elite and public, sacred and secular. Thus, Kathryn Ringrose has aptly labeled eunuchs "perfect servants." (DeFranza, page 74)

There is some debate about whether eunuchs were necessarily castrated or asexual. Some scholars have argued that there were men who assumed the role of eunuch without ever being castrated—taking on only the role, but not the physical transformation. Burke goes to great length to explore both linguistic and socio-rhetorical evidence regarding how universally "eunuch" implied castration or atypical genitalia. Burke concludes that,

> [T]he evidence does not support the repeated assertion of some scholars that in antiquity the word *eunuchos* could be used to refer to a noncastrated court official. (Burke, page 38)

Janet Everhart clarifies further about the eunuch's sexuality:

> Contrary to popular perceptions, the eunuch's inability to procreate does not necessarily include a lack of sexual desire or an inability to perform sexually. Gary Taylor aptly notes that despite the Freudian association of castration with the lack of a penis, castration historically has meant the absence of testicles, the procreative male organs. Indeed, there is ample evidence of eunuchs' sexual involvement with both men and women in a number of different cultures... Eunuchs are often accused of excessive sexual behavior! (Everhart, page 22)

With this complexity of physical characteristic and social role in mind, it is also worth noting that castration was not necessarily voluntary or consensual. Like rape, castration was often used to emasculate, humiliate, and subjugate those who were defeated in battle. Hartke points out,

> Sometimes [castration] served as penalty for a crime or marked someone as a slave for life... Once Israelite and Judean captives were taken as slaves, many were castrated and put into service in Babylonian courts. (Hartke, page 93)

Burke additionally argues that eunuchs were necessarily foreigners and slaves (or freedmen with some obligation to a former master), making "eunuch" a term that denotes not only sex and gender, but also race, class, and nationality:

> [T]wo constituent elements of ancient constructions of eunuchs were slavery and foreignness; in fact, the discourse of foreignness of eunuchs was so powerful that castration could turn a citizen/native into a (fictive) foreigner. (Burke, page 129)

In contrast, Jesus lifts up eunuchs in Matthew 19:12 in a positive way that has had significant impact in the Christian world ever since. We will discuss those developments in the remainder of this section (especially chapters 14 and 17). According to DeFranza,

> Whether intended by Jesus or not, eunuchs came to be associated with angels on account of their (assumed) sexual continence, their freedom from the obligations of marriage (especially its ties to the economic structures of the day), and their alternative gender and gender status. In the Byzantine context, iconography would soon depict angels as beardless and genderless. Hagiographical accounts describe eunuchs and angels being confused for one another on account of similar physical features and dress. Both acted as mediators and messengers for the sacred king, bridging the divide between the sacred and profane. (DeFranza, page 83)

Over time, and especially in light of Matthew 19:12, additional alternate meanings for "eunuch" have emerged. According to DeFranza,

> Given the wider context [of the Matthew text], it is understandable why some modern translations have abandoned the language of eunuch altogether, opting for dynamic equivalents such as those "incapable of marriage" or who have "renounced marriage." (DeFranza, page 72)

Such figurative interpretations of *eunoukhous* are based on a contextual reading of Matthew 19, as Jesus was teaching extensively about marriage just before he mentioned eunuchs (see chapter 14 for further discussion).

Everhart sums up the variety of eunuchs in antiquity:

> [E]unuchs represent a distinct gender that is attested cross-culturally and over several millennia. ... A survey of recent studies of eunuchs in a variety of cultures will demonstrate that, despite cultural variations, the phenomenon of eunuchs is remarkably stable over time. They are typically located near the heart of political and/or religious networks. Eunuchs are liminal, crossing thresholds that present barriers to both men and women. ... Eunuchs are simultaneously respected and reviled, evoking a curious combination of trust and disgust. (Everhart, page 10)

Indeed, Burke argues specifically that "liminality or 'in-betweenness,' was a characteristic of ancient constructions of eunuchs" (Burke, page 126).

Burke offers a survey of the variety of ways that eunuchs were ultimately classified:

> In some discourses, eunuchs are gendered as not-men, effeminate males, or half-men/half-males (*semiviri/semimares*). In others, eunuchs are gendered as girls (*puellae*), or as beings that have actually changed, or are in the process of changing, from male to female. In still others, eunuchs are gendered as hybrids of male and female, or as neither male nor female. In yet other discourses, eunuchs are defined by the loss of masculinity or manhood, or even the loss of humanity itself. (Burke, page 107).

With numerous examples of eunuchs in the Christian Bible, it is striking that so many have been reduced by scholars to being simply "court officials." Burke cites both Orlando Patterson and Gary Taylor to articulate the ways that eunuchs straddled numerous categories in the ancient world: male and female, weak and strong, dirty and pure, sex object and asexual, mother and wife, nature and accident, biology and culture, reality and representation, essentialism and constructionism (Burke, page 120). Burke expands this list with his own additions: free and slave, citizen-or-native and foreigner, penetrator and penetrated (Burke, page 120).

The status of the eunuch as "other" in the ancient world was remarkable even in an ancient context. However, the evolution of the word "eunuch" can be particularly confusing from a modern perspective where we are accustomed to clearly distinguishing biological and physiological features from cultural and social roles, sex from gender, race from nationality. The fluidity of the term "eunuch" has much to teach us about how human identity is constructed—specifically that we are both embodied *and* social creatures.

Our physical form impacts how we are perceived socially. Meanwhile, the social role of "eunuch" also motivates physical transformation (by choice or by force). At the same time, an individual's sense of self influences both how they occupy the role and how they function within their body. "Eunuch" was neither a strictly biological term nor a strictly social one. All three of these factors (biology, social engagement, and individual identity) influence one another in meaningful ways to create a multi-faceted identity like "eunuch."

Even if we assume that the word "eunuch" does indeed point to many different but overlapping identities and experiences in antiquity, the "Terms Paradox" can help us to avoid drawing firm conclusions about specific eunuchs. Yet, we can be sure that every eunuch in antiquity was some sort of OtherWise-gendered human who functioned (for one reason or another) in a middle ground between male and female and outside of the traditional heterosexual marriage, family, and procreative arrangements of their time. As we look back through time, may we find our ancestors smiling back at us from familiar and unfamiliar places.

♡

You are loved. When they do not really understand you. When people are getting all kinds of confused. When they try to forget you are even there. You are loved.

Chapter 12
Modern Day Eunuchs

Let us go forward, then,
to mature teaching
and leave behind us
the first lessons
of the Christian message.
We should not lay again the foundation
of turning away from useless works
and believing in God.

Hebrews 6:1
Good News Translation

John McNeill famously argued in his 1976 classic, *The Church and the Homosexual*, that the "eunuchs from birth" in Matthew 19:12 were "the closest description we have in the Bible of what we understand today as a homosexual" (McNeill, 1993 edition, page 65). This assertion is based on the idea that men who are born without desire for heterosexual sex or marriage are eunuchs in a figurative sense. This figurative reading of the eunuch focuses on the role and expectations of the eunuch rather than the physical embodiment. If we assume that some men were born with homosexual inclinations in the ancient world, then they may have been drawn to the role of eunuch as a way to avoid social expectations of heterosexual marriage that were prevalent at the time.

Nancy Wilson argued provocatively in her 1995 book, *Our Tribe: Queer Folks, God, Jesus, and the Bible* that eunuchs (and barren women) were "*our gay, lesbian, and bisexual antecedents*" (Wilson, page 124). Written in the 1990s, when same-gender civil marriage still seemed like an impossible dream in the United States, Wilson's assertion had significant resonance with the more traditional "incapable of marriage" interpretation of eunuchs in Matthew 19:12. Noting various connections between barren women and eunuchs in the Hebrew text, Wilson suggests that the biblical eunuch may be a metaphor—"a generic term used to refer to men and women who did not or could not produce children" (Wilson, page 123). With Wilson, the emphasis is that eunuchs lack procreative function.

Victoria Kolakowski may be the first published author to identify eunuchs with the experience of post-operative transsexual women in her 1997 article:

> [T]he post-operative transsexual is *agonado*, sexually sterile. A post-operative male-to-female transsexual is thus considered according to [the Western binary] model to be a castrated man, a eunuch. (Kolakowski, "Toward a Christian Ethical Response to Transsexual Persons," page 17)

Kolakowski's emphasis is on the physical act of castration as comparable to gender-affirming surgeries that remove the genitalia (penis and testes) of transgender or transsexual women. This is a much more literal reading in terms of procreative function, even though castration in the ancient world lacked all of the reconstructive aspects of gender-affirming surgeries today.

Prior to Kolakowski's publications, there was an emerging consensus about eunuchs among increasingly unapologetic gay and lesbian biblical scholars. Kolakowski's "The Concubine and the Eunuch" chapter in 1997 was a critical intervention on behalf of transgender communities:

> As a lesbian transsexual Christian, these New Testament stories are extremely powerful statements of validation and acceptance from Jesus and the early Christian Church. This is unlike the message that well-meaning gay and lesbian biblical scholars have been sending—that the Christian Scriptures are simply neutral rather than overly negative about us. I believe they paint a very different picture, one which I am not inventing just to feel accepted. We need to take ownership of this radical message. (Kolakowski, "The Concubine and the Eunuch," page 47)

Were eunuchs gay men who were born that way? Were eunuchs same-gender-loving folk who opted out of the ancient heteronormative-marriage industrial complex? Were eunuchs transgender women in a time before technology and customs had evolved to make viable medical and social transition as we know it today? Well, it is complicated. Equating the identity of "eunuch" with any modern-day experience in the Western world is a stretch simply because the modern Western world is culturally and scientifically so very different from the ancient world. Even if the role or physical features of a eunuch are similar to some of these modern identities, they are not the same.

As mentioned in the previous chapter, DeFranza argues convincingly that the mention of "eunuchs from birth" by Jesus in Matthew 19:12 aligns closely with the historically documented category of "eunuchs of the sun" (*saris khama*) in antiquity—that is, with literal intersex persons born with ambiguous genitalia. "Some intersex conditions, like Klinefelter's syndrome, bring about physical characteristics almost identical to those described of castrated eunuchs in the ancient world" (DeFranza, page 103). DeFranza goes on to highlight the specific symptoms and experience of an individual with Klinefelter's.

Even in this most literal case, "eunuchs from birth" are similar but not the same as people with intersex conditions in the modern world. While the physical variations presenting at birth and through life may very well be identical, people with those atypical birth characteristics are no longer assigned the social role of "eunuch" in the modern world. Therefore, eunuchs are not the same as modern intersex people, just as *hijra* in India are not the same as *waria* in Indonesia. Even though there may be significant similarities, it would be reductive to claim that they are the same, since language, culture, and history play a significant role in any social identity.

Furthermore, some gay men and transgender women bristle at being compared to castrated men. For instance, Timothy Koch (cited by Everhart, page 64) expressed "a great deal of, umm, shall we say, *discomfort*" at the idea that he should identify with a surgically altered eunuch, when such a physical adjustment was neither his experience nor desire. Likewise, Kolakowski acknowledges that modern transgender women are often similarly disturbed by the analogy. "I'm not just a castrated man; I'm a woman," they will argue (Kolakowski, "The Concubine and the Eunuch," page 48).

Identity words are tricky. We would do well to hold tight to the "Terms Paradox" (see chapter 11) as we navigate such analogies and comparisons. Kolakowski argues that gay, lesbian, bisexual, and transgender people as well as eunuchs are

> all "queer," in both the best and worst senses of the word. That's why I find the discussion of procreation and eunuchs so important. The discussion points to the basis of our commonality as sexual minorities. (Kolakowski, "The Concubine and the Eunuch," page 49)

Sidestepping the more specific identity language, I offer that eunuchs *are* a decisive example of OtherWise-gendered identity in the ancient world. Eunuchs are a "gender identity or expression that transcends the simplistic Western settler-colonist narrative of two and only two mutually exclusive and unchangeable genders, defined strictly and easily based on biology at birth" (see chapter 2). Eunuchs were an alternate gender, different from and in-between male and female. A eunuch's identity could be defined based on biology at birth (for example, "eunuchs of the sun"), but they could also be "made" through castration at any later point and for a variety of reasons.

In a modern world where we have been invited (and are often forced) to conform to reductive ideas about sex and gender, the eunuchs of old are most certainly role models for a gender-full resistance. They help us imagine a world where OtherWise-gendered people can function as an acceptable and well-known aspect of society, well-integrated into social, political and religious institutions. Most importantly, as we will see in the coming chapters, eunuchs have often be used by God "for the sake of the kingdom of heaven." Let us move on to consider the biblical testimony in more detail so we can celebrate the stories of many OtherWise-gendered characters who are doing God's work in the world! For we, have been a part of God's story for a very long time.

♡

You are loved. When you are looking for your ancestors. When you are exploring your history. When you are longing for sacred community. You are loved.

Chapter 13
Blessing the Eunuch

Isaiah 56:1–5

Do not let the son of the foreigner
Who has joined himself to the Lord
Speak, saying, "The Lord has
utterly separated me from His people";
Nor let the eunuch say,
"Here I am, a dry tree."
For thus says the LORD:
"To the eunuchs who keep My Sabbaths,
And choose what pleases Me,
And hold fast My covenant,
Even to them I will give in My house
And within My walls a place and a name
Better than that of sons and daughters;
I will give them an everlasting name
That shall not be cut off."

Isaiah 56:3–5 NKJV

In chapter 10 of this book, I examined Deuteronomy 23:1. In that text, whether because of their bodies, their behaviors, their infertility, or simply because of stigma, eunuchs were rejected and devalued. Even though Deuteronomy 23:1 is not consistently applied as a literal prohibition by either Jewish or Christian authorities in the modern day, it does reflect a history where eunuchs were considered marginalized or "less than."

It is with that context in mind that we consider this powerful text from Isaiah 56. Justin Tanis summarizes the passage:

> This passage reveals a new commandment from God that directly contradicts earlier law. Part of the justice that God now demands requires that the people practice an acceptance and inclusion of others in their midst, including foreigners and eunuchs. Not only are such people to be included, but the prophet goes on to declare that God will give them a name better than sons and daughters, an everlasting name. (Tanis, page 69)

Nancy Wilson explains the significance of being included in (or excluded from) such a lineage:

> [F]or most of the duration of biblical Judaism, the primary way one could achieve any sense of "immortality" was through one's descendants, one's children. Through them, you, your life, and your people lived on. ... The worst fate that could befall someone in such a culture and religion was to be *cut off* from one's people. There were three primary ways in which one could be cut off: by being exiled for certain crimes or afflictions, by public execution, or by dying without leaving any children. Those who were cut off were thought of as having been "cursed." (Wilson, page 121)

Conversely, having a name by way of many sons and daughters would be considered a blessing. Having a name "better than" sons and daughters, as Isaiah 56 promises, would be a promise of a very powerful legacy and blessing.

The historical context of the Isaiah passage (5th century BCE) is one where the Israelites had been defeated and taken into slavery (under the Babylonian Empire), probably with some being castrated in the process:

> And some of your sons, your own issue, whom you will have fathered, will be taken to serve as eunuchs in the palace of the king of Babylon. (Isaiah 39:7; 2 Kings 20:18)

The Israelites to whom these passages are addressed were either fearful of becoming or had recently found that they themselves (or their loved ones) had become eunuchs and foreigners under the control of another nation.

In this historical context, the eunuchs and foreigners of Isaiah 56 also functioned as a metaphor for the entire nation of Israel, which had become concerned for its own collective fertility and future in this time of defeat and subjugation. These promises of restoration are for the outcast, but they are also for the Jewish people as a whole. Metaphorically, the eunuch becomes closely associated with and even representative of the larger community. This kind of collective identification and solidarity with the eunuch (and the foreigner) is a far cry from being "cut off" as it shows a deep sense of camaraderie and connection.

Isaiah 56 speaks evocatively of the restoration of eunuchs and foreigners. This chapter is part of a series of images in Isaiah—speaking to the restoration of barren women (Isaiah 54), the hungry (Isaiah 55), and the lowly in spirit and those who mourn (Isaiah 57). As Tanis puts it,

> We see in this section of Isaiah that the divine vision of the world is now one that embraces differences and gathers the outcasts, rather than one that limits, distinguishes, and excludes... God's promises to gather in the

> outcasts and to bring rejoicing to those brought low in society's judgement are promises to all of us. (Tanis, page 71–72)

Lewis Reay calls the promise of Isaiah 56 "an unrestrained revolution to the existing world order of who can approach God" (Reay, page 158). In a contemporary world that continues to make outcasts in so many ways, this is a powerful promise, indeed!

Austen Hartke goes on to note that there is a shift of emphasis in Isaiah, moving from a focus on sorting out individuals to the transformation of the community as a whole:

> God did not ask the eunuchs to pour themselves into the mold of Israel's previous societal norms, nor to bend themselves to fit by taking on specifically gendered roles in the current system. Instead God called for a transformed community that looked like nothing the people had ever seen. (Hartke, page 99)

Beyond the significance of procreation and fertility in the ancient world, Hartke elaborates on how the language of Isaiah 56 also evokes some of the foundational stories of Jewish tradition in terms of the promises made to Abraham and Sarah:

> What God was giving to the eunuchs, through Isaiah's proclamation, was not just a place in society, and not just a hope for the future. By giving the eunuchs the same kind of gifts given to Abraham and Sarah—a name, legacy, family, acceptance, and blessing—God was consciously associating the two stories in the minds of the people. ... Though the eunuchs did not find themselves in exactly the same circumstances as their ancestors Abraham and Sarah, the blessing they received was similar enough to invoke that ancient memory. (Hartke, pages 98–99)

Again, this re-connects the eunuch, not only to community generally, but specifically to the lineage of Abraham and Sarah, and thus to the most honored lineage of the Jewish tradition.

Through the eunuch in antiquity, we can see that OtherWise-gendered people were ridiculed and looked down upon. They were expected to have no future, no legacy, no community. They were to be "cut off." Yet, the turnaround in Isaiah contradicts all of that shame and abandonment with a sense of radical connection to God's sacred people. Despite a history of being despised, Isaiah 56 promises that eunuchs (and barren women and foreigners) will be restored to God's favor.

♡

You are loved. When you are without a name. When you do not like your name. When you change your name. When you claim your name. You are loved.

Chapter 14
Jesus and the Eunuchs

Matthew 19:11-12

But [Jesus] *said to them,*
"Not everyone can receive this saying,
but only those to whom it is given.
For there are eunuchs
who have been so from birth,
and there are eunuchs
who have been made eunuchs by men,
and there are eunuchs
who have made themselves eunuchs
for the sake of the kingdom of heaven.
Let the one who is able to receive this
receive it."

Matthew 19:11–12
English Standard Version

Back in the day, there were flyers titled, "What Jesus said about Homosexuality." When you opened them up, the inside was blank. Later, this argument would take the shape of blog entries and even attempted memes. However, Jesus really did have something significant to say about OtherWise-gendered people. He specifically identified three different kinds of eunuchs in Matthew 19:12—and this is where it gets really juicy!

According to Victoria Kolakowski,

> The third category [eunuchs for the sake of the kingdom of heaven] is not found in any pre-Christian source and is generally believed, by even the most skeptical scholars, to be original to Jesus. ... [H]e created a third category of the procreatively deviant, those made eunuchs for the sake of the kingdom, which he clearly implies includes himself. The radicalness of this lifestyle should not be overlooked or influenced by our modern acceptance that not having children is an acceptable life choice. (Kolakowski, "The Concubine and the Eunuch," page 44)

Even though the original Matthew 19:12 text uses eunuch (*eunochoi*) three times, the Contemporary English Version refocuses the text around marriage:

> Some people are unable to marry because of birth defects or because of what someone has done to their bodies. Others stay single for the sake of the kingdom of heaven. Anyone who can accept this teaching should do so. (Matthew 19:12 CEV)

By reducing the meaning of "eunuch" to someone who does not participate in traditional heterosexual marriage, the interpreter removes all of the rich historical context related to Jesus using the world "eunuch."

As Justin Tanis puts it,

> Many scholars argue that this passage is not to be taken literally, but refers primarily to those who have foregone marriage and become celibate in order to better serve the church. Jesus' intention was clearly broader than that, because he includes not only people who abstain from marriage but all possible configurations of eunuchs. Limiting Jesus' teaching solely to celibates oversimplifies this passage and does not hold us, as the community of faith fully accountable to the extent of Jesus' words. (Tanis, page 73)

Focusing on the unmarried aspect of the eunuch's role is in some ways congruent with Jesus' earlier teaching in that chapter of Matthew around marriage and divorce, but the "unmarried" interpolation leaves out a great deal that would have connected this teaching to Jewish tradition(s) around eunuchs—from Deuteronomy 23:1 (and elsewhere) dismissing eunuchs as inferior if not immoral (see chapter 10) to the promise in Isaiah 56 of restoration for the eunuch who serves the Lord well (see chapter 13). Jesus was steeped in Jewish tradition, so it seems unlikely that he would have used "eunuch" reductively to mean "unmarried."

Since Jesus is usually believed to have been unmarried and celibate, we can imagine that he would have had firsthand experience with the religious and cultural stigma against eunuchs. These personal dynamics add additional layers of meaning to the teaching of Matthew 19:12. Victoria Kolakowski notes,

> It is frequently argued by those who hold that Jesus was celibate that Jesus himself had been derisively called a eunuch, and that it was this charge to which Jesus was responding in this statement, placing himself into the third category. The notion that Jesus placed himself into the third category makes this passage particularly fascinating... since it would place Jesus in direct solidarity with the eunuch. ... [T]here is no condemnation

> of eunuchs implicit in this statement; rather, Jesus is placing himself into an analogous situation with the eunuchs. (Kolakowski, "Toward a Christian Ethical Response to Transsexual Persons," page 25)

In terms of sexuality, Janet Everhart summarizes the eunuch's sexuality:

> [E]unuchs in a variety of cultures are associated with non-normative sexual behavior. Eunuchs can have sex without procreating; some eunuchs are sexual partners of both men and women. (Everhart, page 9)

Even if celibate himself, Jesus was a man of the world who spent time with sex workers (also known as prostitutes). Surely, he would have been familiar with the reputation of the eunuch in matters of sexuality—and aware that aligning himself with eunuchs in this way would be quite provocative!

Nancy Wilson calls this Matthew 19:12 verse "the most *under commented on* in all the Gospels" (Wilson, page 128). She goes on to note:

> It is amazing to me that: neither the story of Philip and the Ethiopian eunuch, nor the story of Ebed-melech in Jeremiah, nor Isaiah's prophecy in Isaiah 56 are cross-referenced in the New RSV with Matthew 19—or *any* Bible or standard commentary! These are the politics of biblical interpretation at their most subtle and at their worst. Such gross omission and silence obscure the possible relationship of these passages. (Wilson, page 128)

It remains provocative to this day that Jesus identified with OtherWise-gendered people. A significant portion of Christendom is still invested in the idea that Jesus was gendered as the Son, a man, a patriarch of either asexual or "vanilla" inclinations. For many Christians, thinking of Jesus as being in any way "freaky" like the eunuchs of old simply does not compute.

However, taking Jesus' teaching literally in terms of thinking about castration is by no means a 21st century invention of gender activists. Taking Jesus' use of the word "eunuch" seriously dates to the early church. Austen Hartke summarizes:

> As it turns out, some early Christians did take these verses at face value, either in their own lives or in their teachings, and did choose to either castrate themselves or to live outside the boundaries of their assigned sex, or both. ... The long and the short of it is that some early Christians did exactly what Jesus hinted at here, and the practice of castration as a form of religious devotion became common enough that when the Council of Nicea was called in 325 CE, the very first rule they made barred anyone

> who had willingly been castrated from becoming a clergyperson. (Hartke, page 106)

In chapter 17 of this book, I will look in more detail at ideas about eunuchs in the early Christian Church and how the meaning of "eunuch" continued to evolve as a result of Jesus' teaching in Matthew 19:12.

Hartke goes on to unpack more about what "becoming a eunuch" would mean in terms of the power dynamics of the day:

> By making themselves eunuchs, Christian men in the early church were intentionally giving up power they held as men in their culture. They were taking an action with the direct consequences of placing themselves lower in the social hierarchy. (Hartke, page 107)

As discussed in chapter 4 of this book, all humans were considered men, with superior and inferior expressions. Manly men were at the top; women and children were at the bottom; and alternate genders such as eunuchs were somewhere in-between. A man who changes into a eunuch (whether literally by castration or figuratively by abstaining from marriage) moves down this hierarchy as he gives away (some of) the power of his masculinity.

This relinquishing of privilege is particularly interesting in light of the overall flow of Matthew 19. While Matthew 19 begins with the teaching on marriage and divorce, once Jesus mentions eunuchs, he proceeds immediately to a teaching about how the kingdom of heaven belongs to children (Matthew 19:14). So his discussion moved neatly from the top of the hierarchy (married men) to somewhere in the middle (eunuchs) to the bottom (children).

As Matthew 19 continues, Jesus offers teachings on giving up wealth (Matthew 19:16–24) and family/inheritance (Matthew 19:25–29), which are additional factors in one's privilege and social safety net. The chapter ends with the well-known phrase, "But many who are first will be last, and many who are last will be first" (Matthew 19:30 NIV). Reading Matthew 19:12 as a text about sex, gender, and all of the meanings of "eunuch" fits just as comfortably into the overall context of Matthew 19 as does the reductive "unmarried" interpretation—and arguably more so.

Justin Tanis points to the overall arc of Jesus' ministry among outcasts and outsiders as a further connection:

> This understanding of Jesus seeing himself as analogous to eunuchs also fits with his identification with others on the margins of society. ... This statement about eunuchs would not be the first time that he placed himself in connection with outcasts. In fact, we could argue that a modern parallel to the tax collectors and sinners might be spending time with drag

> queens and bikers, people seen as outside decent society and social norms. (Tanis, page 75)

Yet, in his ministry, Jesus demonstrated no need to "heal" or "correct" those with atypical bodies, such as "eunuchs from birth" or "eunuchs that were made so by men." Neither does Jesus make any distinction between those who asexually abstain from marriage (in other words, the unmarried celibates) and those with non-normative sexual practices beyond the bounds of heterosexual marriage (in other words, the sexually active, but unmarried eunuch). Moreover, there is never an admonition that the eunuch must repent in order to be a part of the kingdom of heaven.

Kolakowski summarizes her reading of Matthew:

> I believe that the word *eunuch*, applied to Jesus, was as derogatory and hateful as the word *Queer* is in modern times... But Jesus took that derogatory slang word thrown at him and proudly claimed it as a part of his own identity. ... Jesus' saying here was an "in-your-face" comeback, and it was so shockingly powerful that his followers remembered it and later wrote it down. (Kolakowski, "The Concubine and the Eunuch," 1997, pages 44–45)

Matthew 19:12 places Jesus right at the center of our conversation about OtherWise-gendered people in the Christian Bible. This verse shows that Jesus was not only knowledgeable about gender variance in antiquity but that he had no apparent qualms about it either. Indeed, we see Jesus aligning himself quite closely with eunuchs, perhaps based on his own personal experience of stigma against the unmarried. Jesus goes so far as to offer the eunuch as emblematic of the kingdom of heaven in a way that would shape Christian culture for centuries to come. With this kind of testimony from the mouth of Jesus Christ himself, it is no wonder that church scholars might want to avoid connecting the words of Jesus with literal eunuchs or the assorted eunuchs that appear elsewhere in the Bible. However, by focusing only on marriage, modern scholars have reduced Jesus' proclamation to something much less powerful than it actually is. Let us give thanks for the eyes to see and ears to hear. Let us receive these gifts and give thanks!

♡

You are loved. When they do not believe what you said. When they ignore what is right in front of them. When they refuse to take you seriously. You are loved.

Chapter 15
Two Ethiopian Eunuchs

Jeremiah 38:1–13 and Acts 8:26–40

However,
Ebed-melech
the Ethiopian,
a eunuch
who worked in the royal palace,
heard that they had put [Jeremiah] *in the well.*

Jeremiah 38:7a
Good News Translation

Upon this [Philip] *rose and went.*
Now, as it happened, an Ethiopian eunuch
who was in a position of high authority
with Candace, queen of the Ethiopians,
as her treasurer,
had visited Jerusalem to worship there.

Acts 8:27
Weymouth New Testament

There are two significant stories involving Ethiopian eunuchs in the Christian Bible—the story of the prophet Jeremiah being saved by Ebed-melech (Jeremiah 38:1–13) and the story of the nameless Ethiopian eunuch baptized by Philip (Acts 8:26–40). The Acts 8 text is easily the most well-known reference to a eunuch in the Christian Bible, while Ebed-melech's story is a relatively unknown text. According to Janet Everhart, "[B]iblical scholars have rarely connected the stories" (Everhart, page 170).

In my experience, actor and playwright, Peterson Toscano, has done the most to raise awareness about the story of Ebed-melech among contemporary Christians. In his "Falling for Ebed Melech" chapter, Toscano tells the story of "the Other Ethiopian Eunuch" (though it is even more fun to watch him perform the story, so check the bibliography for a YouTube video):

> Jeremiah calls on the nation to repent or else suffer the consequences. Instead of heeding the warning, some in the ruling party capture the prophet, drag him into the palace, drop him into an empty muddy well, and leave him there to die.
>
> King Zedekiah, who is sympathetic towards Jeremiah, doesn't have any real power in the court to help his friend. Perhaps someone who is often overlooked in the palace can assist? Enter Ebed Melech. This Ethiopian eunuch goes directly to King Zedekiah and urges action. As a result, the King of Judah gives Ebed Melech some fighting men so they can rescue Jeremiah.
>
> Ebed Melech organizes a Special Ops midnight raid to "Navy-seal" Jeremiah out of the muddy well and the palace. This foreign-born court official thinks of everything, including rope to haul Jeremiah up from the well. The rescue team also bring with them old rags. These the eunuch tosses down to the prophet and whispers, "Put these rags under your arms, so when we pull you up, the rope won't cut or burn your skin." This Ethiopian eunuch saves the old man prophet. This often overlooked Black, African, surgically altered, and gender variant eunuch becomes a savior. (Toscano, 2017, page 21)

In the next chapter, in anticipation of coming disaster, God gives Jeremiah a prophecy—a promise that Ebed-melech will be rescued by the Lord: "[Y]ou will not be given into the hands of those you fear. I will save you; you will not fall by the sword but will escape with your life, because you trust in me, declares the LORD" (Jeremiah 39:17b–18 NIV). While this promise is specifically for Ebed-melech, it also echoes the promises made in Isaiah 56 to eunuchs and foreigners who serve God faithfully.

The Acts 8 story of the Ethiopian eunuch is much better known, as the story of the first Christian baptism. Unfortunately, this prominent Ethiopian eunuch remains nameless. Noting the complications of constantly referring to the "Ethiopian eunuch" by their gender and nationality (perceived as race in the modern day), Tolonda Henderson calls the main character "the traveler" (Henderson, page 15). I will follow suit, which will also help distinguish between the traveler and Ebed-melech (both being Ethiopian eunuchs).

The Acts story is rich in nuance and significance, as Philip meets a traveler on the road from Jerusalem. Justin Tanis (citing F. Scott Spencer) notes that the setting of the story is rather extraordinary. In Acts 8:26, the word *mesembrian* is often translated "south," but literally means "midday." Traveling at midday in a desert climate would be atypical and dangerous. More importantly, they were in the wilderness on the road from Jerusalem to Ethiopia. This would be a reverse of the Exodus journey that the

Israelites took from Egypt to Jerusalem, giving this location in transit further religious and cultural significance:

> The fact that the eunuch encounters Philip in the midst of all of these "between" spaces affirms the workings of God outside of human boundaries and conventions. In fact, this encounter is made possible in part by the unusualness of the space and time in which they encounter one another. (Tanis, page 78)

After Philip and the traveler discuss a text from Isaiah 53 and then the "good news of Jesus" (Acts 8:35), the traveler becomes the first Christian baptized in the early church (Acts 8:36–38). The details provided about the traveler become almost as important as the story itself. Everhart (citing Cottrell R. Carson) notes "this is the longest introduction of any person in the [New Testament] except for Jesus" (Everhart, pages 175–176). Long story short, the traveler was "a quadruple threat" (Hartke, page 115) as an outsider on several counts, including nationality/ethnicity, religion, class, and gender.

The traveler is described as an Ethiopian (or Cushite). In other words, he was from present-day Ethiopia or Eritrea on the African continent. While white pastors and theologians often allow "the Ethiopian eunuch" to become a generic, almost meaningless, label for an unnamed character, many African-American Christians have a special love for the traveler who would also become the patron saint of the Christian church in Africa. While an "Ethiopian" would be considered "Black" by today's standards of race, at the time "Ethiopian" would have primarily communicated that the traveler was a foreigner (without all the extra layers of racial identity that would emerge centuries later under North American white supremacy). Being a foreigner would still mark the traveler as an "other."

In the context of the Luke-Acts storyline about spreading the gospel throughout the world, it matters that the first baptism was the baptism of a foreigner as it extends salvation decisively beyond the nation of Israel. According to Hartke (citing M. B. Kartzow and H. Moxnes), Ethiopia was "a place that was considered 'the ends of the earth' in that day and was a military threat to the Roman Empire" (Hartke, page 114). So Ethiopia was not a near neighbor or ally, but a far-away land, perhaps considered an enemy of the state. If you are in the United States, you might think of Ethiopia as being like Russia, Iraq, or North Korea. The newly baptized traveler would take the gospel message with him to this far-off place.

Tanis (citing F. Scott Spencer) acknowledges that the traveler is "somewhere between Jew and Gentile, worshiping in Jerusalem but from

Ethiopia" (Tanis, page 78). The traveler's religious perspective placed him in between and again marked him as an outsider. Hartke suggests that the traveler was

> what the Bible calls "God-fearer," which essentially means a person who ascribed to the beliefs of the Jewish people despite not having been born among them. This placed him in between or outside of the established categories when it came to the Jew/Gentile binary of the times. ... [H]e was neither a Jew by birth nor a full convert. (Hartke, page 115)

This story is a key transition point between earlier portions of Acts that occur among Jewish communities and later portions of Acts that occur among the Gentiles. Again, the baptism of the traveler represents an expansion of the early church's vision for Christian community.

The traveler was a person of great authority in the court of Queen Candace, trustworthy enough to be responsible for the funds of her kingdom. Yet, as a eunuch functioning in a foreign court, it is very likely that the traveler was also a slave. As a highly valued servant with enough independence to make his way as far as Jerusalem, the traveler once again embodies an in-between status, neither slave nor free.

As discussed in chapter 11, the traveler being described as a eunuch does not necessarily tell us whether he was a "eunuch from birth," castrated or simply functioning in the non-procreative role of a eunuch. According to Victoria Kolakowski, "In this case, however, scholars appear to agree unanimously that he was castrated" (Kolakowski, "The Eunuch and the Concubine," page 23), in part because he is identified as both a eunuch and a high ranking servant of a queen. If he was only fulfilling the role of a eunuch, then calling the traveler a eunuch would have been redundant.

Sean Burke points out that the critical question in this story happens around the baptism, "What can stand in the way of my being baptized?" (Acts 8:36 NIV). Burke quips: "The audience knows that there are many reasons to prevent the eunuch from being baptized" (Burke, page 137). He's a eunuch! He's a foreigner! He's not a Jew! Burke does an extensive analysis of the traveler's various identities, concluding that even the ambiguities of his identities are not a problem (in need of a solution), but rather central to telling the story of a eunuch as someone who transcends boundaries (Burke, page 119). What we do not know or cannot tell about the traveler is part of what makes him important to the story of an all-inclusive, Christian community that has no regard for such distinctions. According to Kolakowski and Tanis,

> The radicalness of this story lies in the fact that the early Christian Church appeared to think that baptizing a eunuch was nothing so important as to

> be even be worth discussing. No moral condemnation is implied. (Kolakowski, "Toward a Christian Ethical Response to Transsexual Persons," page 46)

> The power of this story lies in its specific description of inclusion. He is not baptized in spite of being a eunuch or after a lengthy session of apologetics explaining his gender to Philip, but simply at the point at which they passed a body of water. (Tanis, page 79)

In their 1997 article, "Transexual Theology," Starchild points out that Philip doesn't take much convincing in order to expand the gospel vision beyond the Jewish people. By contrast, it takes a much larger conversation (and vision) before Peter endorses a similar approach in Acts 10. Who could become a Christian was a key question in the early church and in the book of Acts. Hartke makes a finer point of the dual conversion by connecting it to the continuing work of the church today:

> In a way, the story of Philip and the [traveler] is a story about two conversions. The [traveler] may be the one who gets baptized, but Philip is the person who has to change his metric for who's in and who's out. Even though this story is two thousand years old, a third conversion is still taking place: will the church eventually realize that when God's love overpowers all human distinctions, nothing can prevent us from full inclusion? (Hartke, page 127)

In the beginning of the Acts 8 story, Philip meets the traveler as the traveler is reading from the prophet Isaiah in a way that is evocative of Luke 4:16–21 (where it was Jesus who was reading from Isaiah). This time, the text is from Isaiah 53:7–8, which talks about being "cut off"—something that may have caught the traveler's attention (and ours) as a metaphor for the plight of the eunuch. The Isaiah 53 text is in the same section as the Isaiah 56 text (discussed in chapter 13), which promises restoration for the eunuch and the foreigner. As these various details converge, we do not get a picture of the traveler as an isolated outsider or as an exception to the rule at all. Rather, the eunuch's story appears to be woven deeply into the overall story of God's people through the ages. This is particularly remarkable since the crowds were "furious" with Jesus in that same section (Luke 4:24–29) after he spoke of mercy for foreigners:

> In contrast, Philip and the [traveler] *enact*, in the wilderness, the kind of inclusive community that Jesus suggests in Luke 4. The foreign eunuch is included without conflict or question. (Everhart, pages 184–185)

According to Everhart, "Jerome may have been the first Christian reader to note, for posterity, that two Ethiopian eunuchs appear in the Christian canon" (Everhart, page 173). However, it remains uncommon for the two texts to be read together. Nancy Wilson playfully calls out this on-going oversight as "*eunuch phobia*" and "*Ethiopian phobia*," (Wilson, page 129) though she does not elaborate further on how the stories might be connected.

Everhart builds on the work of James M. Scott and Cottrell Ricardo Carson in her reading of these two stories, emphasizing that Ebed-melech and the traveler show more agency than any other people labeled eunuchs in the canon. They were both serving in a royal court and are presumed to be slaves. Nonetheless, both Ethiopian eunuchs are portrayed as having direct access to their rulers, as well as significant freedom of movement. Both had connections to Jerusalem and were remarkably assertive in engaging with faith leaders in their respective stories. They each played an extremely positive role in resolving the issues of their day. While Ebed-melech took initiative in saving Jeremiah, the traveler took initiative in asking to be baptized.

Everhart notes, "The eunuchs in these stories are doubly 'other,' as Black foreigners who are also castrated men" (Everhart, page 173). She continues, "Identified as both 'foreign' and 'eunuch,' the Ethiopian eunuchs appear to be doubly eligible for Isaiah's promise in 56:3–6" (Everhart, page 178). According to Burke's analysis (see chapter 11), there was basically an assumption that any "eunuch" would also be slave and a foreigner. The stories of Ebed-melech and the Acts 8 traveler are the most detailed stories of eunuchs that we have in the Bible—and in each of these stories, we see Burke's thesis in action.

Eunuchs may be "other" or "freaky," "ambiguous" or "confusing," or maybe even "queer," but they are also getting the job done! Both of these characters are celebrated as models of faithfulness. Ebed-melech receives a promise of physical rescue as a result of his service, while the traveler receives the blessing of baptism. In each case, salvation is come, and the Isaiah 56 prophecy is fulfilled. These beloved foreign eunuchs are not just tolerated but honored and embraced by God.

♡

You are loved. When you have come from a mighty long way. When you are not sure that you belong. When you are faithful and claim the promise that has been given. You are loved.

Chapter 16
A Flock of Eunuchs

Blessed also is the eunuch
whose hands have done no lawless deed,
and who has not devised wicked things against the Lord;
for special favor will be shown him for his faithfulness,
and a place of great delight in the temple of the Lord.

Wisdom 3:14 NRSV

The 42 mentions of eunuch (*saris*) in the Hebrew scripture make for a whole story book full of OtherWise-gendered folk saving prophets and nations. As Nancy Wilson put it, "the Bible is virtually swarming with eunuchs!" (Wilson, page 125). These stories are ripe for further research and reflection on how the "eunuchness" (Everhart, page 41, citing Peter Guyot) of those characters may provide additional insight into the stories.

The Eunuchs of Esther

The Book of Esther

The book of Esther is especially full of eunuchs who are called by name. Peterson Toscano famously portrays the eunuch, Hegai, in his play, *Transfigurations: Transgressing Gender in the Bible*, but there are a total of 11 or 12 eunuchs listed by name as we move through the book of Esther. We first meet Hegai in Esther 2:3 as Queen Vashti has rebuffed the king's advances (made through seven other eunuchs listed by name in Esther 1:10–11). Hegai was in charge of preparing new virgins for the king, while another eunuch, Shaashgaz, was in charge of the concubines (Esther 2:14). In the midst of various shenanigans, Esther is put under the care of Hegai (Esther 2:8) and gains the king's favor, in part by following Hegai's advice (Esther 2:15).

With Mordecai's help, Esther uncovers an assassination plot by two other eunuchs, Bigthana (possibly the same as Bigtha in Esther 1) and Teresh (Esther 2:21 and 6:2). We also meet Hathak who was one of Esther's eunuch messengers (Esther 4:4–17). In Esther 6:14, the king's eunuchs retrieve Haman for the banquet and, as the drama reaches its climax, the eunuch, Harbona, proposes a fitting end for Haman (Esther

7:9). As Toscano notes, this flock of eunuchs personally facilitates a great deal of the drama unfolding in the story of Esther:

> Yes, Esther saves the people by appearing before the king pleading her case, but without the eunuchs she would have been far from the court, an unknown orphaned Jewish young woman. ... She needs eunuchs to ferry messages back and forth, to set up the lunches for the king, to help her save her people. (Toscano, 2013)

Eunuchs in Community

The Book of Jeremiah

We have already met Ebed-melech, the Ethiopian eunuch who saves the prophet Jeremiah (see chapter 15), but, elsewhere in Jeremiah, eunuchs are noted as part of the community that goes into exile (Jeremiah 29:2). In Jeremiah 41:16, the remnant saved by Johanan includes "men of war, women, children, and eunuchs," and, in Jeremiah 52:25, a eunuch had been placed in charge of the warriors. While eunuchs are often portrayed as "soft" or "effeminate" and as having roles among the womenfolk, it is clear that at least some of Ebed-melech's kindred eunuchs (if not Ebed-melech, himself!) were also military leaders working among the men. Similarly, in 2 Kings 18:17, the king of Assyria sends his chief eunuch among his military leaders with a great army against Jerusalem.

Janet Everhart elaborates on the often obfuscated role of eunuchs in the military:

> Although most English translations of the Bible [in Jeremiah 52:25 and 2 Kings 18:17] render *saris* as "officer," I can find no reason other than contemporary assumptions about masculinity and power to identify this *saris* differently from his counterparts in other places in the biblical text and in other parts of the [ancient Near Eastern] world. The cross-cultural data... clearly demonstrated that eunuchs served as military commanders in a variety of cultures. Biblical writers depict them in similar positions, but translators have tried to remove them! (Everhart, page 145)

Two Eunuchs

Between Jezebel and Jehu

In 2 Kings 9:32–33, two or three eunuchs have the dubious honor of casting down Queen Jezebel as the ruthless King Jehu approaches the city of Jezreel. Just as two soldiers on horseback defected from support of the ruling family after being sent to inquire of Jehu (2 Kings 9:17–20), these two or three nameless eunuchs betrayed Jezebel in favor of Jehu (this time to a gory and gruesome death with blood everywhere). In the grand scheme of the Hebrew text, such a betrayal may be interpreted as being faithful to the new king chosen by God's prophet. However, in such a reading, it really does not matter that they were eunuchs.

Victoria Kolakowski provides a deeper analysis by assessing the significance of the gender dynamics involved. The text leaves us unclear about the motivations of the eunuchs, though they were certainly caught in the middle of the politics of the day—forced to choose between the once powerful Queen Jezebel and King Jehu, the newly usurping king (who is apparently known for driving like a madman!). For Kolakoski, Jehu is in charge, but hardly a hero in this story, as he represents blustering strength without virtue. For instance, he shows a lack of ethics by shooting King Joram and King Ahaziah in the back. Meanwhile, feminist scholars have described Jezebel as the "quintessential foreign woman of power" (Kolakowski, 2000, page 105, quoting Fewell and Gunn) who is demonized because she does not submit. Neither King Jehu nor Queen Jezebel is portrayed as admirable.

With those gender dynamics in mind, Kolakowski argues that "[t]he eunuchs are a wild card in the story" (Kolakowski, 2000, page 103). Perhaps the eunuchs simply chose the winning team, but they also revealed the impotence of Jehu's bluster by showing that he needed help from "unmanly" men to defeat the powerful and allegedly devious Queen. Unlike Ebed-melech, these eunuchs receive no reward for aligning themselves with Jehu's impulsive (perhaps toxic) masculinity. Kolakowski closes by reflecting on the temptation of assimilation:

> Dominant power does not thank others for submission; submission is presumed. Submission is a survival technique, and as long as that is necessary, then there is no real incorporation at all. In spinning new stories and meanings for ourselves, we need to question whether we are doing so to thrive, or merely to survive. (Kolakowski, 2000, page 112)

Daniel and Three Men

The Book of Daniel

In Daniel 1:3, we meet Ashpenaz, the chief eunuch of Babylon (in the service of King Nebuchadnezzar). The king sends Ashpenaz in search of promising young Israelite men, who would be trained for three years before becoming servants of the king (Daniel 1:3–5). Among those selected to be in training under the chief eunuch were Daniel, Hananiah, Mishael, and Azariah, who would be given the Babylonian names, Belteshazzar, Shadrach, Meshach, and Abednego, respectively.

The text states that Jerusalem had just been conquered (Daniel 1:1) and that there was a guard over the men (Daniel 1:11), indicating that they were treated as captives or slaves. These men of Judah would have been foreigners in the Babylonian court, and none are reported to have been married. While the text does not specify that these men were castrated, and they are not referred to as eunuchs directly, they definitely fit the profile of the eunuch in antiquity. It is hard to imagine that young men of that time and place in this situation would be spared from castration, but there is no doubt that they were at least functionally eunuchs since they were prepared for service specifically by Ashpenaz, the chief eunuch of the court.

Since the text is written from a Jewish, not Babylonian, point of view, it is easy to imagine that the author simply avoided mentioning castration in order to avoid making explicit the stigma associated with eunuchs. In fact, Isaiah 39:7 and 2 Kings 20:18 predict that sons of Israel will be "taken to serve as eunuchs in the palace of the king of Babylon" (see chapter 13). To the sympathetic reader, young men such as these may remain captured noblemen of Israel despite being conscripted into a perhaps humiliating role as slaves in Babylon—just as shame may prevent some parents from talking about a beloved child's transition. Indeed, Daniel becomes a legendary hero for surviving the lion's den (Daniel 6), as do Shadrach, Meshach, and Abednego for surviving the fiery furnace (Daniel 3). Like the Ethiopian eunuchs discussed in chapter 15, these eunuchs have been celebrated through the ages for their remarkable faithfulness against all odds.

Blessed Eunuchs and More

The Wisdom of Solomon (or Book of Wisdom) is considered canonical by Roman Catholic and Eastern Orthodox Churches, though Protestants call it apocryphal. In Wisdom 3:14, we see an echo of Isaiah 56 with a promise made to eunuchs—a promise of blessing, a promise of special favor, and a promise of great delight. Barren women are similarly lifted up in the adjacent Wisdom 3:13, making this episode further reminiscent of the section of Isaiah that we explored in chapter 13.

As if that is not enough, there are a few more passing mentions of eunuchs functioning in eunuch-typical roles—messenger (1 King 22:9), a court official (2 Kings 8:6), and people in care of royalty (1 Samuel 8:15). In chapter 19, I will come back to the eunuchs who show up in the midst of

Joseph's sojourn in Egypt (Genesis 37:36ff.). That is before we even begin to speculate about the hidden eunuchs who may not be identified with the specific Hebrew word, *saris*. There are other words in Hebrew for military leaders, court officials, counselors, leaders, and servants who could have been eunuchs without being noted explicitly as such. For instance, Obadiah was steward of the king's household (1 Kings 18:3), and Nehemiah was cup-bearer to a king (Nehemiah 1:11b). They could easily be eunuchs hiding in plain view. Then there are all of the other magicians, soothsayers, and prophets (many nameless) who may or may not be eunuchs.

While we cannot say for sure about every instance, there are enough people specifically labeled eunuchs in the Bible for us to know that OtherWise-gendered people were a familiar feature of the time. We can also see that OtherWise-gendered people have served faithfully in the family of God through the ages in a variety of roles. We have seen that OtherWise-gendered people can be powerful—capable of leadership and prophecy, of loyalty and service, as well as betrayal and assassination. While frequently viewed as secondary characters, eunuchs are people who get caught up in all kinds of power dynamics as they mediate and modulate between different people and places, sometimes making critical decisions that change the course of history.

♡

You are loved. When you are powerful. When you are prophetic. When you are hiding in plain view. You are loved.

Chapter 17
Eunuchs for the Sake of the Kingdom

[A]*nd* [Jesus] *said,*
"Truly I say to you,
unless you are converted
and become like children,
you will not enter
the kingdom of heaven."

Matthew 18:3
New American Standard Bible

In considering the teaching of Jesus about the eunuchs in Matthew 19:12 (see chapter 14), Virginia Mollenkott cites Luke 17:21, where Jesus teaches that "the kingdom of God is within you." Mollenkott then suggests that becoming a eunuch "for the sake of the kingdom of heaven" means looking within to be "true to one's deepest nature" (Mollenkott, 2007 edition, page 136). This may seem like a decidedly modern reading, though it makes good sense of the Greek *entos* (in Luke 17:21), which means "inside" or "within" (even though it is sometimes translated "in your midst"). Actually, similar themes have emerged in Judaism, including "Go to yourself" as a literal translation of God's command to Abraham (*lekh lekha* in Genesis 12:1) and Hillel's famous quote, which begins "If I am not for myself, who will be for me?" God's handiwork is written deep within each of us and we connect to God's purpose in our lives when we find and honor that sacred core.

However, that was not a prominent interpretation in the early church. Not only was the Matthew 19:12 verse about eunuchs influential, but it was read in connection with the subsequent section, Matthew 19:16–29, which advocates for relinquishing both possessions and family connections. Megan DeFranza notes,

> In the early church, "eunuchs for the sake of the kingdom" came to be understood as those who were willing to leave behind the burdens and earthly joys of family, in the hopes of everlasting reward. While most manuscripts of the Gospel list only siblings, parents, and children [in Matthew 19:29], early Christians soon added "wife" as the most pivotal renunciation of all. The associations and responsibilities of family life (marriage, sexuality, children, inheritance, ownership of property) came to

> be viewed as the evil powers of the "present age." (DeFranza, pages 82–83)

In Matthew 18:3, Jesus teaches about becoming like little children, which resonated with the pre-pubescent features of eunuchs (particularly those castrated before puberty) as well as the Matthew 19:14 affirmation of children. Eunuchs also became associated with angels, the divine messengers and go-betweens. DeFranza notes,

> Jesus' teaching on eunuchs—read through the lenses of children, angels, and sacrifices for the kingdom—radically altered the way eunuchs have been understood in the West. Rather than elite slaves or castrated (but sexually active) priests of Cybele, eunuchs came to signify non-castrated but sexually continent priests and the castrato singers of the church—perfect servants of the King of kings. Free from the fetters and distractions of family, innocent and asexual as children and angels, with angelic voices that raised audiences to the heavens—eunuchs were transformed from the immoral other into a new model of Christian perfection. (DeFranza, page 83)

In Christ Jesus, both women and men were initially encouraged to pursue celibacy, with gender distinctions declining in importance. Tertullian (2nd and 3rd century CE) perhaps represents the unfolding views of the time. He used "eunuch" as a slur, but also taught that Jesus "stands before you, if you are willing to copy Him, as a voluntary eunuch in the flesh" (DeFranza, page 86, citing translation by Mathew Kuefler). Note that the Greek here is *spado*, not *eunuchos*. Scholars have suggested that *spado* refers to castration of both penis and testes (Kuefler, page 33), in contrast with *eunuchos* which only involves the testicles. In any case, Tertullian does not specify in what way Jesus being a "voluntary eunuch in the flesh" relates to literal castration.

There was also a prominent tradition in the early church that took Matthew 19:12 literally. Origen was a prolific writer and early church father who functioned parallel to Tertullian (2nd and 3rd century). Origen is infamous for his (literal) self-castration. According to Eusebius, Origen castrated himself in order "to be a eunuch for the kingdom," though other traditions cite motivations relating to controlling his libido (Kolakowski, "Toward a Christian Ethical Response to Transsexual Persons," footnote 26, citing Kodell). Tensions between understandings of Matthew 19:12 as referring to literal or figurative eunuchs persisted for some time.

Voluntary castration was strongly discouraged at the Council of Nicaea (325 CE), and, in 393 CE, Origen was condemned as a heretic. This was also the time when Christianity was shifting from persecuted sect to the official religion of the Roman Empire, leaving little room for ambiguity about which Christian teachings would be enforced. Over time, the idea of "spiritual eunuchs" began to replace literal (castrated) eunuchs in Christianity. According to Mathew Kuefler,

> Spiritual eunuchs might be virgins, continent persons, men or women in sexless marriages, or widows. The variety of interpretations, all related to sexual renunciation... [included a] willingness [by] the Church fathers to refer to women as well as men as spiritual eunuchs. (Kuefler quoted by DeFranza, page 94)

Augustine (4th and 5th century CE) would rail against the *galli* (castrated priests of Cybele) in particular. As literal (castrated) eunuchs were increasingly demonized, the distinction between manly men and unmanly men once again became prominent, as did the distinctions between men and women. Monasteries "set down rules that boys, eunuchs, and beardless men were not to be admitted. It was believed that the androgynous beauty of eunuchs and boys would tempt other monks into sexual sin" (DeFranza, page 97).

Views in the Eastern church changed around the 8th century CE as castration was again normalized, and literal (castrated) eunuchs appeared in prominent religious positions as well as politics for several centuries. In the West, castrati singers were appreciated in the church, but literal eunuchs would not otherwise return to prominence. To the degree that literal eunuchs became associated with virtue and holiness in these later periods, the category of manliness was expanded to include eunuchs. In other words, the concept of eunuch was transformed from an altogether alternate gender into simply an alternate kind of masculinity.

My treatment here is necessarily cursory, although the gender, sexual, and theological dynamics are nuanced. I am following Megan DeFranza, who in turn summarizes Kathryn Ringrose (and others). According to DeFranza's summary,

> Jesus' positive evaluation of eunuchs... transformed the discussion of eunuchs into a declaration of the virtues of the virginal life. ... The metaphorical eunuch became the new icon of Christian perfection... both East and West distanced the eunuch from its origins as a representative of androgyny, reconstructing the eunuch as a model of manliness. Perfection, even Christian perfection, continued to be construed as a ladder of ascent toward manliness. (DeFranza, pages 101–102)

What seems most extraordinary to me about this history is just how hard Christians through the centuries have worked to make sense out of Jesus' teaching on eunuchs. In doing so, they explored and experimented. They stepped away from cultural norms (inside and outside the church), time and again, as they sought to be more like Jesus. Many of their conclusions were influenced by patriarchy, misogyny, and toxic masculinity, but I find it inspiring that Christian history is full of diverse and contradictory opinions about what it means to be a "eunuch for the sake of the kingdom of heaven."

Equipped with modern day perspectives on gender, class, and liberation, we, too, have the opportunity to rethink what it means to be OtherWise-gendered in the service of the King of kings! We are not bound to ancient models of slavery, royalty, or manliness, any more than the early Christians were. It is our turn to make sense of one of the most provocative teachings of Jesus. We do know that "Jesus was undermining the power structures of his day: family ties, inheritance of wealth and property, gender privilege" (DeFranza, page 105), but it is up to us to be in discernment about how we might respond to similar power structures of our time.

Like the early Christians, we, too, are called to pick up this mantle—to envision a Christian practice that is grounded in the liberating work of Jesus, to build a Christian community that is based in mutuality and sharing power, and to share a Christian story that undermines the forces of oppression in our present day. Praise God for this challenge and this opportunity!

♡

You are loved. When you are ready to flip the script. When God makes a way where there was no way. When you are joining the upside down kingdom. You are loved.

SECTION FIVE
OtherWise Jewish Tradition

Chapter 18
Torah Study

The LORD had said to Abram,
"Leave your native country,
your relatives,
and your father's family,
and go to the land that I will show you."

Genesis 12:1
New Living Translation

Here I am,
a stranger and
a foreigner
among you.

Genesis 23:4a
New Living Translation

So what then does an OtherWise Christianity look like? We learned in our review of the eunuchs that gender, class, and nationality are often intertwined with religion and culture—which can in turn dramatically impact the way we perceive tradition. OtherWise Christianity means working to be culturally competent, in general, but also more specifically in regards to our roots in Judaism. Cultural competency is a topic that extends beyond the scope of this book, but I have found Joy Ladin's recent work to be a powerful counterpoint to many Christian misrepresentations of the Jewish tradition.

I already touched on issues around Creation in chapters 6–7 and Mosaic Law in chapters 9–10. In her book, *The Soul of the Stranger: Reading God and Torah from a Transgender Perspective* (still a new release that, as I write this, is deserving of more attention), Ladin also touches on several familiar stories from Torah (what Christians consider the first five books of the Hebrew scripture), including Abraham, Sarah, Isaac, and Jacob/Israel. In so doing, Ladin further develops her argument that our gender is not nearly as important to God as is our humanity (mentioned briefly in chapter 7).

Ladin's approach is radical insofar as she holds to *pshat*, a plain reading of the text. She holds to the fundamentals of text and tradition without depending on complicated academic theory or literary criticism to find new meaning. In doing so, she provides fresh insight from a traditional reading:

> In reading the Torah from a transgender perspective, I am not trying to "queer," "trans" or otherwise reimagine the text. Like the rabbis, I believe that all interpretations, including those from [the transgender] perspective, are already planted in the Torah, waiting for us to discover them, and like the rabbis, I believe that new interpretations add to rather than compete with traditional understandings. (Ladin, *The Soul of the Stranger*, page 11)

I understand Ladin to be saying that new insights need not invalidate previous interpretations of the text at all. Christians have much to learn from the multivocal nature of Jewish tradition, which encourages engagement with many layers of meaning in the text, rather than just one, singular and superficial reading. Ladin elaborates as she discusses the Book of Jonah:

> I don't mean to suggest that the Book of Jonah is about being transgender. The Book of Jonah is about being human. But transgender experience is human experience, and questions transgender people face are questions that we all face. Everyone, transgender or not, has to decide what parts of ourselves we will and will not live. Each of us has to decide when we can't and when we must sacrifice our individuality for the sake of our families and communities, when we have to be what others count on us to be, and when, like Jonah, we have to live the truths that set us apart from others and reveal to the world what we have only revealed to God. (Ladin, *The Soul of the Stranger*, page 7)

Ladin is not arguing that these Bible characters were "transgender" as we understand that word today but, rather, that they had human experiences (often around the gender constructs of their time) which are relatable for those of us who are transgender today. She goes on to explore gender roles and expectations as they influence several key characters in Jewish tradition.

The story of Abraham begins already in Genesis 12 as Abraham (then Abram) is called by God to leave his elderly father behind, to go away from his relatives, and to depart from his native land in order to travel into the unknown of the wilderness. Ladin notes that God pointedly calls Abraham away from the obligations of his assigned gender as the firstborn son of Terah. In following God's command, Abraham is abandoning his family of origin and all of the obligations that he would have carried as a firstborn son:

> On the one hand, Abraham becomes a firstborn who acts like a second-born by leaving his father's house rather than remaining as his support

> and heir; on the other hand, Abraham becomes a patriarch whose inheritance (God's promised blessings) and status come not from his father, but from God. (Ladin, *The Soul of the Stranger*, page 43)

The transformation of Abram into Abraham continues in Genesis 17, as God gives Abram a new name and commands genital surgery for all of the men in Abraham's household, as a sign of the new covenant between God and Abraham's people. Ladin argues that this, too, represents a transformation of Abraham's gender:

> Abraham's abandonment of his firstborn role was a private, family matter. His name change publicly signifies that he has become a different kind of man, a kind of man who had never before existed... a Jewish man, a man whose circumcised body attests to his covenant with God. (Ladin, *The Soul of the Stranger*, page 45)

Sarah (originally Sarai), the wife of Abraham, is also transformed in relationship with God. After Hagar, a servant, becomes Abraham's concubine and pregnant with his child, Ishmael, Sarah lashes out in frustration (Genesis 16). As a barren woman, Sarah experienced what Ladin calls a "gender failure." As a result of lifelong infertility, Sarah was not successful in providing an heir for Abraham as was expected of women in that culture. Some rabbis went so far as to speculate about whether Sarah had a womb at all (making her what we might call intersex), but, whatever the cause of her infertility, the text makes it clear that Abraham and Sarah having a child together was laughable (Genesis 17:16–17). Even sexual relations at their advanced age seemed absurd, according to the text (Genesis 18:12).

Nonetheless, God gives Sarah a child at the advanced age of 90. While Sarah remains a woman, she is no longer barren; she is no longer the same kind of woman as she was before God intervened:

> Sarah's pregnancy makes her a kind of woman who cannot be understood in terms of [standard mother] roles at all. According to binary definitions, Sarah can either be [an] old woman or a new mother, but not both. By making her a kind of woman who... is impossible, Sarah's pregnancy demonstrates God's presence in her life and in the world. (Ladin, *The Soul of the Stranger*, page 50)

This miracle turns Sarah into a gender bender, not just because of her unexpected transition from barren woman to fertile woman but because she simultaneously occupied two categories that were thought to be mutually exclusive—new mother and old woman.

As a result of this hilarious conception, Sarah and Abraham's child is named *Yitzak* (Isaac), which means laughter. Yet, in Isaac's story (Genesis 22), we confront the painful impact of religiously justified violence within the family unit as Abraham nearly kills Isaac, believing that it was or would be God's will. In reflecting on Abraham's willingness to do such harm, Ladin points out the impact of gender-based violence within a family system,

> turning family members into mortal enemies who see us not as cherished children, siblings, parents, or spouses but as creatures that must be sacrificed, a nightmare in which we cannot even cry out to God, because it is God, we are told, who demands that we be targeted. (Ladin, *The Soul of the Stranger*, page 56)

Ladin notes that sacrificial gender roles impact even those who, like Isaac, are faithful to their assigned gender roles. Ladin further suggests that, despite Isaac's continued obedience, this incident would forever damage Isaac's relationship both with his father and with God:

> For Isaac, Abraham's willingness to step outside of the role of father does not make him a liberating example of the ways God can lead us beyond gender; it makes him a monster. ... Modern commentators often read [this story] as a story not of Abraham's triumph but of his failure. ... According to this view, God hoped that Abraham would reject God's command, and reject any relationship with God that would require him to kill his son. (Ladin, *The Soul of the Stranger*, pages 58–59)

Ladin's reading of Jacob (and Esau) parallels her reading of Abraham insofar as she focuses on the social location of firstborn sons, but this story also turns on the different masculinities of these twin brothers. Esau is the first twin to emerge and is thus assigned the role of firstborn son by a margin of a few minutes. Esau is also portrayed as more masculine in contrast with Jacob who is more effeminate in appearance, in temperament, and in relationship with their parents (Genesis 25).

Jacob imitates Esau's clothing, hair and even smell in order to gain the blessing of his now blind and ailing father, Isaac (Genesis 27). Only Jacob's voice betrayed his scheme, leaving Isaac with a sense of discomfort and unease. As Ladin notes, Isaac depended on secondary gender markers to distinguish between his sons, making gender pivotal in this power play. As Ladin summarizes,

> the misrecognition in this scene represents more than Isaac's personal failure, and more, even, than the danger of relying on the external signs of gender to identify other people: it represents the triumph of God's will

> over human gender. ... No matter how strongly we sympathize with Isaac's and Esau's betrayal and disappointment, disapprove of Jacob's fraud, or believe that when it comes to gender, biology is and should be destiny, if we identify ourselves with any of the religions and cultures that grew out of the Torah, then we have to root for Jacob to succeed in impersonating his brother and becoming the kind of man he was not born to be. (Ladin, *The Soul of the Stranger*, pages 41–42)

Thus, Ladin traces three generations of Jewish founding fathers through their relationship with birth order and related gender expectations. Abraham abandoned the role of firstborn. Isaac was a dutiful second child (after Ishmael), but was nearly killed as a result. Jacob (who would later become Israel) steps into the role of firstborn late in the game by a gender-full deceit which displaces his older brother. In each case, Ladin notes that God is right there in the midst of the action, actively undermining humanity's established gender roles and expectations.

Ladin writes poignantly about the tension many of us feel as we navigate between family expectations and the need to express our true selves. She goes on to examine Jewish practices around the Nazarite vow (Numbers 6) as another example of how Jewish tradition balances individual vocation and community obligation:

> These laws authorize "anyone, man or woman" to determine their own lives, as long as they do so in the specific way and for the sake of a relationship with God. ... Like many transgender people today, those who took Nazarite vows changed their behavior and appearance in ways that violated social norms, marking themselves as different and setting themselves apart from those around them. ... According to Jewish law, someone could become a Nazarite at any time, without any preparation or explanation. ... [T]he Nazarite laws not only tell Nazarites what to do; they also make it clear that God expects other Israelites to accept the self-determination of those who take Nazarite vows. (Ladin, *The Soul of the Stranger*, pages 108–109)

Ladin bravely acknowledges that rejecting one's assigned gender can have a negative impact on others in one's family and community. She invites us to lean into that tension with God's blessing:

> These [Nazarite] laws acknowledge that even acts of self-determination that disrupt our families can be sacred. They make it clear that the God who speaks the language of patriarchy and binary gender throughout the Torah also empowers individuals to leave the roles and identities we are born to and set ourselves apart for the God who dwells in the wilderness beyond them. (Ladin, *The Soul of the Stranger*, page 112)

Ladin offers many other insights and reflections on these and other texts. I will review the concept(s) behind her title in chapter 21, but I want to acknowledge one more thing about the "father of many nations" here. In Genesis 23:4, Abraham identifies as both stranger and foreigner. Abraham's departure from his assigned gender and from his family of origin is what starts him on his sojourn into other lands. This transformation from firstborn to wandering stranger/foreigner also connects him to our eunuch friends (chapters 11–17) who some argue were made into forever-foreigners by virtue of castration.

Ladin does a remarkable job of bringing a fresh perspective to classic patriarchal texts, arguing that gender is a versatile tool to be used as God sees fit:

> God in the Torah uses gender, but is not bound by it. ... The Torah presents gender as a means to God's ends, to be reinforced or disrupted as God pleases. ... [I]n these stories, faithfulness to gender has little to do with faithfulness to God. In fact, God counts on the fact that people are not bound by gender roles. (Ladin, *The Soul of the Stranger*, pages 57–58)

While Ladin does not flinch from evidence of patriarchy and misogyny within Jewish tradition, her thoughtful reading shows that God is not concerned with such constraints. Among her closing thoughts, Ladin offers this beautiful charge to the OtherWise-gendered of the world:

> [E]very time, the Torah refers to God as the God of Abraham, Isaac, and Jacob, it helps me remember that even trans experiences that cut us off from other people can connect us to God. But the horror of [Isaac's near sacrifice] reminds us that relationship with God is not enough. When we enter the wilderness of possibility beyond the gender roles we have been born to, it is up to us to maintain the moral values that are normally bound up with those roles: to be faithful even when we are seen by others as betrayers; to take care of those who depend on us even when they feel we have abandoned them; to be good even when we are seen as evil; to be loving even when we are objects of hatred; to hold ourselves to the highest standards even when others don't value us at all. ... [E]ven when it is God who leads us into the wilderness, it is up to us to decide what it means to be human. (Ladin, *The Soul of the Stranger*, page 60)

May each of us be found faithful as we journey through our own wilderness.

As someone raised in Christian tradition, I am especially grateful for the ways that Ladin's work has helped to liberate me from caricatures that portray Jewish tradition as overly concerned with roles, rules, and regulation, leaving no room for individuality. Those of us who are Christian have so much to learn from our Jewish siblings, especially those who are OtherWise-gendered. Thanks be to God for these many gifts!

♡

You are loved. When you are fulfilling your obligations. When you are changing your appearance. When your life seems laughable and absurd. You are loved.

Chapter 19
Joseph(ine)

Genesis 37–50

Now Israel loved Joseph
more than any of his other sons,
because he had been born to him
in his old age;
and he made [a]
[ketonet passim] *for him.*

Genesis 37:3 NIV
with transliteration added

Joseph is one of the most explicitly genderqueer characters in the Bible. In Genesis 37:2 (also Genesis 41:12), Joseph is described as a *na'ar*, a boy or a lad. *Na'ar*, in this context, is typically understood to mean that Joseph was working as a servant, since a 17-year-old was already considered a man in that time. Such an idiomatic use of *na'ar* reminds me of how full-grown African-American men are frequently called "boy" in white supremacist society in order to infantalize them and "put them in their place." The idiom places an expectation of submission and subservience.

Gregg Drinkwater in his contribution to *Torah Queeries: Weekly Commentaries on the Hebrew Bible* points to an additional layer of meaning in *na'ar*.

> In the midrash, the sages suggest that although Joseph was indeed seventeen, he "behaved like a boy, penciling his eyes, curling his hair, and lifting his heel" (Genesis Rabbah 84:7). ... Calling Joseph a boy is a way of feminizing him while questioning his emotional and social maturity. Calling him a *na'ar* also contrasts him starkly with his brothers, who are clearly understood as adults. (Drinkwater, page 54)

Using *na'ar* places Joseph among the eunuchs (and other servants), women, and children as unmen (see chapters 4 and 11). Physically, Joseph is described as beautiful (Genesis 39:6b), in exactly the same way as his mother Rachel (Genesis 29:17). The text also tells us that Joseph was a tattle-tale (or a drama queen?), regularly reporting back to Israel about the inadequacies of his brothers and others in his father's household.

Joseph's "coat of many colors" (also "technicolor dreamcoat") is a well-known image from one of the most detailed stories in all of scripture. However, despite the familiarity of this special robe, scholars variously describe Joseph's robe as everything from "difficult to translate" to "shrouded in mystery." An NIV footnote says, "The meaning of the Hebrew for this word is uncertain." Scholars who go into more detail will note that the Hebrew phrase, *ketonet passim*, also appears in 2 Samuel 13:18–19 as the robe of Tamar (the daughter of King David). As they speculate on the meaning of this phrase, scholars examine similarities between the two stories and usually conclude that the robe is ornate, worn by royalty, and too lengthy to be suitable for manual labor.

In his 2005 book, *Jacob's Wound: Homoerotic Narrative in the Literature of Ancient Israel*, Theodore W. Jennings Jr. offers a much simpler explanation. Like Joy Ladin in the last chapter, Jennings holds to *pshat*, the plain reading of the text. In 2 Samuel 13:18b, the text itself describes the robe as "the kind of garment the virgin daughters of the king wore" (NIV). In other words, this robe was a woman's garment. This interpretation was popularized by Peterson Toscano in his play, *Transfigurations: Transgressing Gender in the Bible.* Toscano points out that the virgin daughter of a king is typically referred to as a "princess," so Toscano lovingly dubs the ornate, long robe, a "princess dress."

The only thing "difficult" about such a plain reading of the phrase, *ketonet passim,* is the way it challenges the assumption that all of the patriarchs were manly men. As Toscano goes on to unpack the rest of the story with this princess dress in mind, he dramatically takes on the role of Joseph's manly uncle, Esau, with caricatured masculinity. Toscano reminds us that Esau's brother Israel (originally named Jacob) was described in Genesis 25 as being physically effeminate, as being closer to his mother, and as dwelling in the tents with the women. In short, Israel was quite the ambitious "girly boy" in his younger days. Now a patriarch and father of 12 sons and one daughter (by four different women), Israel honors his favorite son, Joseph, with a princess dress made by his own hand—leaving the remaining brothers not jealous, but hateful toward Joseph.

Initially, the brothers intended to kill Joseph for his petulance. Instead, they rip the princess dress, throw Joseph in the bottom of an empty well, and sell him to a passing caravan as a slave. While placing Israel's and Joseph's less masculine gender expression at the center of the story is not the only option that makes sense out of this violent family history, it is an approach that resonates deeply for anyone who has ever been called a "sissy" by a schoolyard bully or who has otherwise experienced "gay-bashing." There is a peculiar kind of rage in the brothers' treatment of Joseph, as well as their focus on his princess dress. We know well that patriarchal masculinity is often threatened by "unmen" who are not sufficiently submissive. In light of the princess dress, it seems that Joseph was being punished for wearing a woman's garment, for being too close to his effeminate father, for being a different kind of man (an unmanly man), and for not being sufficiently deferential to his older brothers.

J Mase III extended Toscano's insights in his spoken-word piece, "Josephine (What the Bible Says about Transfolk)" which was first released in a YouTube video in 2013 and is excerpted here:

> I want to know from you
> Have you heard the good word about
> Joseph of Genesis?
> See
> Joseph
> Josephine
> Jo of Genesis
> favorite child of Jacob
> Aka Israel...
>
> Jo
> when your brothers saw you
> in your flowing dress
> in all your glory
> they became enraged
> I am sorry for the beating you received
> Sorry they destroyed your dress
> and smeared it with the red paint of your swollen veins
> Josephine

J Mase III, "Josephine" (excerpt)
text provided by the author

Mase's poetic retelling of the story also serves to question Joseph's gender by playing with his name, "Jo, Joseph, Josephine." While this move certainly takes poetic license, it also presses the question, "What kind of man wears a princess dress?"

As a result of the drama with his brothers, Joseph is cut off from his family and made a slave in a foreign land. While it would seem rash to call Joseph a literal eunuch, it is not a stretch to say that Joseph's predicament resonated with what many of our eunuch friends would have experienced (see chapters 11–17). In a sense, the brothers were putting Joseph in his place—the place of a eunuch. Depending on where the caravan carried him, Joseph could easily have been at risk of castration as an already effeminate young man who had just been sold into slavery. He did, in fact, become a foreigner and a slave who was cut off from his family of origin—arguably because of his gender expression, as represented by that princess dress.

According to Genesis 37:36 (and Genesis 39:1), Joseph was eventually sold to Potiphar, who was a eunuch (*saris*) and captain of the guard in Egypt. Again, scholars tend to avoid the most obvious reading by arguing Potiphar could not be a literal (castrated) eunuch because he was married. However, the situation is reminiscent of the way that the prophet Daniel and his friends were placed in the care of the head eunuch in Babylon. Who better to take on an inexperienced eunuch-like slave than a leading eunuch in the service of the Pharaoh? Joseph did well serving in the household of Potiphar and was given a great deal of responsibility.

Genesis 39 tells us that Potiphar's wife made numerous sexual advances toward Joseph—which leaves us wondering why she was apparently so dissatisfied in her marriage. While there is some debate among scholars of the ancient world as to whether or not castration was practiced in Egypt, a plain reading of the text tells us that Potiphar was (at least) a figurative eunuch. If being a eunuch meant that Potiphar was an asexual or same-gender-attracted man, then Potiphar probably didn't bring any sexual interest to his marriage, and it would make sense that Potiphar's wife might go looking elsewhere. As an experienced warrior, it is easy to speculate that Potiphar might have had war injuries pertinent to his eunuch status. Eventually, the drama with Potiphar's wife landed Joseph in prison, with two more eunuchs—this time, the chief cupbearer and chief baker—who had upset the Pharaoh (Genesis 40:1–3).

In subsequent work (some published, some not), Mase identifies Joseph as a survivor of familial violence. Mase reminds us that intimate violence has lingering impacts on survivors, including anxiety and sleeplessness. Like many survivors, Joseph never seems to discuss his history of being violated. The fictions created by his brothers and later by Potiphar's wife are believed without question by those who should have been Joseph's protectors. In every case, Joseph seems to suffer in silence, rising above assault and slander by caring for those around him. Mase places a very personal spin on this aspect of the story's violence and we are hopeful that further publications will be forthcoming to elaborate on his insights around related dynamics.

Like Daniel, Joseph was an interpreter of dreams who would go on to become a valuable advisor to the Pharaoh. Joseph would also marry an Egyptian woman and have two sons (which makes it clear he was not castrated upon his arrival in Egypt). As the story unfolds, Joseph is eventually reunited with his family of origin during a time of extreme famine.

Joseph would have been more than justified in retaliating against his brothers, and he had more than enough power to make them pay a steep price for their betrayal, but Joseph chooses subtlety, over the obvious—restoration over retribution. Joseph carefully manipulates the circumstances around the arrival of his brothers and, finally, we see Joseph's pain, as he weeps on seeing his younger brother, Benjamin, for the first time in years (Genesis 43:30). Joseph sets aside the trauma and betrayal he endured, providing forgiveness and generous hospitality to his family of origin in their time of need. This is how the 12 tribes of Israel came to dwell in Egypt.

Loved ones are not always able to protect OtherWise-gendered people from the demands of the world—or even from the rest of the family. We learn to hold our pain close as we negotiate our way through awkward, if not violent, family situations. Joseph shows us that we are not the first to endure such disregard and that we have choices about how we deal with our pain. Indeed, our experiences of rejection and trauma may eventually equip us to do a better job of caring for and protecting others.

♡

You are loved. When you get hurt. When the weeping comes. When the pain never seems to go away. You are loved.

Chapter 20
Virile Women and Trans-Masculine Experience

The LORD is my light
and my salvation—
whom shall I fear?
The LORD is the stronghold
of my life—
of whom shall I be afraid?!

Psalm 27:1 NIV

So far, our consideration of OtherWise scripture has been almost exclusively concerned with men—manly men, castrated men, first-born men, effeminate men—and a few earth beings. In her analysis of Rebekah, Rachel Brodie begins by quoting Yair Zakovitch, a "legendary" professor, who would begin his lectures with, "In the Bible, women are rarely born, they almost never die and when they give birth it is usually to a boy" (Brodie, page 34). This bias toward the insignificance of women (beyond their relationships with men) means that we also have very little evidence in the Bible regarding OtherWise-gendered characters who were assigned female at birth (AFAB). Yet, trans-masculine characters are not entirely missing from the Bible.

Rebekah

Genesis 24

In Brodie's contribution to *Torah Queeries*, she takes a closer look at the Hebrew that describes Isaac's wife, Rebekah. In Genesis 24, we meet Rebekah after Abraham sends his servant to find an appropriate wife for Isaac. According to Brodie,

> Rebekah is not a typical woman of the Bible, partly because of her "masculine" traits (physical strength, stamina, bold social behavior, and independence). Through the eyes of Eliezer the servant, the Biblical text itself seems to approve of the blending of stereotypically masculine and feminine traits. (Brodie, page 35)

Rebekah is described as attractive (Genesis 24:16) but also strong enough to quickly draw adequate water for all ten of the servant's thirsty camels (Genesis 24:20). She was socially independent enough to talk to an unfamiliar man and invite him to be a guest of her household (Genesis 24:17–25).

Brodie explains that Rebekah is referred to as *na'ar* in this chapter. This *na'ar* is the same diminutive word that served to feminize Joseph—portraying him as a boy or a lad. Yet, in this case, it is used for a woman (who would go on to become Jacob/Israel's mother). This *na'ar* designation occurs not once, but five times in regard to Rebekah in this chapter.

Brodie goes on to explain that between the 7th and 10th centuries CE, the Masoretes standardized the Hebrew text, sometimes adding notes or adjustments in the process. The original Hebrew does not include vowels, so the Masoretes would make vowel additions to assist with reading the text aloud as a way to preserve the oral tradition. With regard to these five *na'ar* references, the Masoretes replaced *na'ar* with *na'ar'ah*, which clarifies Rebekah as a young woman who is eligible for marriage. The addition of that one additional (vowel) character does indeed align Rebekah with the rest of the story in terms of being the kind of person the servant was seeking, but the original text without vowels is unclear.

According to Brodie, a *na'ar'ah* would be "especially vulnerable to unwanted sexual attention and should therefore remain close to home" (Brodie, page 36). Yet, we find Rebekah off at the well on her own, accepting gifts from an unfamiliar man. In Genesis 34, Dinah (also *na'ar* replaced with *na'ar'ah*) ends up being raped while wandering in a similarly unattended manner; not so with Rebekah. It is possible that *na'ar* was used as a gender-neutral term to suggest an emergent youth who has not yet been identified according to the distinctions of adult gender. Similarly, given Rebekah's character, we can imagine that *na'ar* may have functioned like the English word "tomboy," indicating a youthful gender ambiguity that included both masculine and feminine aspects.

According to Brodie, there is a tradition of deriving additional meaning from Masoretic adjustments, such as these. The Malbim (19th century CE scholar) and Rav Soloveitchik (20th century CE scholar) both suggested that each side of such a word replacement may hold meaning. In this case, *na'ar/ah* could suggest that Rebekah's visible gender may have been different from her internal sense of self—again consistent with a reading of "tomboy" or trans-masculine gender non-conformity. Unfortunately, the Masoretic adjustment means that the OtherWise ambiguity of both the original *na'ar* and *na'ar/ah* is obscured by the standardized reading of Rebekah as simply an eligible young woman (*na'ar'ah*).

Until Isaac prayed for her to conceive (Genesis 25:21), Rebekah had been barren for 20 years—much like her mother-in-law Sarah. In a particularly unladylike move, Rebekah argues with God about the pregnancy saying, "Why is this happening to me?" (Genesis 25:22). Rebekah is the only woman in Genesis that presumes to engage directly with God. For instance, Eve and Sarah each respond to God, but only after God initiates the dialogue. In contrast, Rebekah approaches God with her question in a way that foreshadows her son Jacob's future wrestling with God (for which he would be given the name Israel). Rebekah's question is ambiguous in Hebrew and is alternately translated as "What will become of me?" (God's Word translation) or "I'm not so sure I want to be pregnant!" (New English Translation) or "Why do I live?" (New Heart English Bible).

The word *le'nokhah* is usually translated to mean either that Isaac prayed "on behalf of" Rebekah or that he prayed "in front of" her (suggesting that they were near one another, possibly praying together). Given Rebekah's response to the pregnancy, I am noticing that *le'nokhah* can also mean "opposite" or "over against" (as in 1 Kings 20:29 where enemy forces are camped "over against" one another). In *Womanist Midrash: A Reintroduction to the Women of the Torah and the Throne*, Wilda Gafney quips,

> It defies credulity to believe that the most active matriarch in the canon never offers a prayer on her own behalf during each of the twenty years in which the reader must imagine that she and Isaac looked and hoped for a child. (Gafney, 2017, page 49)

But, what if Rebekah did not want to be pregnant in the first place? For many trans-masculine people, pregnancy (or even menstruation) can be an extremely dysphoric experience. I am not finding anything in the text to suggest that Rebekah longed for a child. That is something we assume because of her gender and culture and because of Isaac's prayer.

In any case, God does not seem offended by Rebekah's brazen question. Rather, God responds with another nation-making promise. While God's promise to Abraham was confirmed on Isaac (Genesis 26:3–4), it is Rebekah, not Isaac, who receives this inheritance. She will be the parent of two nations (Genesis 25:23). It is remarkable how Isaac fades into the background once Rebekah establishes a direct relationship with God. It is as if Rebekah, the boy/maiden, supplants Isaac as the recipient of God's blessing, taking the agency and initiative to pass that blessing along to Jacob.

While the tradition frequently speaks of God's promises to Abraham, Isaac, and Jacob, it is Rebekah who becomes instrumental in the unfolding story of God's covenant with Israel in this generation. According to Tikva Frymer-Kensky in *Reading the Women of the Bible: A New Interpretation of Their Stories*,

> [Rebekah] is... a second Abraham, who, like him, voluntarily chooses to leave Mesopotamia for Canaan. ... The voyage from Mesopotamia to Israel was the one qualification that Abraham sought in a daughter-in-law, and her willingness to do so establishes her credentials. ... Like Abraham, [Rebekah] is the bearer of the promise. ... "Inheriting" goes from Abraham to [Rebekah] to Jacob and to the people of Israel. Her decisiveness, her strong will, and her embrace of her destiny make her a strong active link between Abraham and Jacob. (Frymer-Kensky, page 13–14)

Rebekah gives birth to the wrestling twins, Esau and Jacob. Rebekah's cunning shows through as she supports the effeminate Jacob in usurping his more masculine brother Esau's birthright (see chapter 21) and then as she manipulates Isaac into protecting Jacob from Esau's revenge (Genesis 27:43–28:5). Jacob would then go to live in the household of Rebekah's brother Laban for 20 years, where he would marry Rebekah's nieces, Leah and Rachel. When Jacob arrives in Harran, he identifies himself matrilineally as the son of Rebekah (Genesis 29:12), reflecting Rebekah's matrilineal origins (in Genesis 24:28, Rebekah runs to tell her "mother's household"), not as the son of Isaac (Gafney, 2017, page 46).

The power dynamic between Rebekah and Isaac is even more intriguing if we follow the Kabbalistic teaching that "Isaac was born with the soul of a woman" (Reb Mikhl Zlotshever and Chaim Ibn Attar, the Or ha-Hayyim, as translated by Abby Stein). In a related reflection, Jay Michaelson notes that Isaac is not only managed by Rebekah, but was also managed at an earlier point by his father Abraham (see chapter 18). Not only does Isaac submit to being sacrificed by his father, he also allows his wife to be chosen by his Abraham's servant. Michaelson provocatively begins to explore the gender and power dynamics between Isaac and Rebekah (Michaelson, pages 54–57), though I am eager for a more in-depth consideration of Rebekah's part in the pairing. Kabbalistic discussion tends to focus on Isaac and I do not want to drift too far away from my focus on Rebekah. Nonetheless, Rebekah, the boy/maiden, and Isaac, the man with a woman's soul, seem to have been an OtherWise match made in heaven.

At every turn, Rebekah seems to embody incongruity. She is the *na'ar/ah* that is both boy and maiden. It is not clear that Rebekah even wanted to be a parent, but she becomes a mother of multiple nations. She bears these twin brothers, one distinctly masculine and one distinctly effeminate. She bucks tradition by favoring the more effeminate and second-born of her two sons. She deceives and manipulates her husband and is outspoken, even to the point of arguing with God. Rebekah is the

OtherWise instrument that God uses to birth, bless, and preserve the one who would become Israel.

Deborah

Judges 4–5

Deborah (Judges 4–5) is another OtherWise-gendered character who has been brought to life by actor and playwright, Peterson Toscano in his play, *Transfigurations: Transgressing Gender in the Bible.* According to Toscano, Judges is one of the bloodiest books of the Bible, taking place after the Exodus but before the kings of Israel. The judges were charismatic leaders who typically came to power by leading Israel to victory in battle. Out of the 12 judges of Israel, Deborah was the only woman.

In this story, Deborah and Yael are a study in contrasts with both women contributing to Israel's victory. While Deborah gains acclaim through her pursuit of traditionally masculine leadership, Yael, a tent-dwelling woman (Judges 5:24), finds glory serving Israel in a particularly feminine way. Yael lures the leader of the opposition army into the intimate space of her tent (Judges 4:18). She offers him milk, a symbol of maternal nurture, and invites him to rest under her care (Judges 4:19). While Yael's stake in the head of Sisera (Judges 4:21) is a rather gruesome part of the story, Yael's betrayal while the military leader lies in her bed is a more traditional example of woman-power in the ancient world. She is a literal *femme fatale.*

In contrast, all of the judges of Israel were political and military leaders operating in the public sphere, and Deborah was arguably the most effective judge Israel ever had. The nation enjoyed 40 years of peace as a result of her leadership (Judges 5:31). While we do not know how she became a judge, we do know that she was already a judge before the described battle, which is a contrast with other judges who clearly became judges after they led Israel to a military victory. Deborah did not have power as a result of her intimate access to a powerful man. She was not respected because of her family, her parents, her children, or because of who she married. She may not have even come to power through military leadership. She was a respected leader because of her virtue, strength and wisdom. As highlighted by Gafney in *Daughters of Miriam: Women Prophets in Ancient Israel,*

> [Deborah] is certainly exceptional in terms of her character... Block concludes that Deborah is the only judge "the narrator casts in an unequivocally positive light," in addition to being the only judge already in

> divine service before being called up for military action. (Gafney, 2008, page 93)

That is all we really need to know to understand Deborah as an OtherWise-gendered character. Deborah seems to function as a typical head of state and commander in chief. However, those considered lesser beings (see chapter 4), such as women, eunuchs, and children, were not typically trusted with such important matters of state, nor would they operate so independently. Clearly, Deborah was different. Deborah is not the stereotypical "virtuous woman" described by so many (citing Proverbs 31) as an industrious and faithful homemaker for her husband and children. As Toscano puts it, Deborah was "not your typical Jewish mother."

While Deborah is clearly identified as a woman throughout the text, there is nothing to indicate that anyone was concerned or surprised about her gender. She was probably considered a virile woman, a masculine or manly woman in her time. Like boys who become men, a woman like Deborah might "move up the ladder toward manly perfection" (DeFranza, page 114) by displaying *virtus*, the kind of virtue which defined a man (*vir*). In later Greco-Roman times, such a woman might be called a *virago*, which could serve as either a pejorative or a complimentary label. While functioning as a man meant a virago was perceived to be closer to male "perfection," it was also considered a kind of gender deviance (Burke, page 71). While these views of women and virago were particularly well-developed in later Greco-Roman thought, ancient Jewish perspectives were not so different in terms of the subordination of women.

Unlike the other warrior-judges of Israel, Deborah is also a prophet (Judges 4:4). According to Frymer-Kensky, this was a role that women often played in the Assyrian region (Frymer-Kensky, page 48). Deborah is respected as a spiritual leader and a counselor, not just a warrior-leader. She is acknowledged as someone who can speak on behalf of God. Indeed, Deborah is one of seven notable prophet-women of Israel identified in the rabbinic tradition. Meanwhile, the Song of Deborah (and Barak) is noted as one of the preeminent poetic works of the Jewish people, alongside the songs of Moses, Joshua, David, Solomon, and more.

Scholars like Frymer-Kensky and Tammi J. Schneider argue that there is some ambiguity to the phrase *ēšet lapîdōt* used to describe Deborah in Judges 4:4. The typical translation domesticates Deborah as the wife of a man named Lapidot. However, *ēšet lapîdōt* is literally "*lapîdōt*-woman." In other words, "woman" and "wife" are so closely connected that they are conflated in the Hebrew. Furthermore, Schneider notes that "*ōt*" is a feminine abstract ending for *lapîd* (meaning torch), which makes it less likely a man's name (Schneider, page 66). According to Frymer-Kensky,

> *Lappîdôt*, "torches," comes where we would ordinarily expect a husband's name, but it is a strange-sounding name for a man and, moreover, does not have the standard patronymic "son of." ... "[W]oman of torches" or "fiery woman" fits the image of Deborah and would fit the story in the manner of biblical names. (Frymer-Kensky, page 46)

Deborah works closely with General Barak, whose name means "lightning." Frymer-Kensky further notes that "in Mesopotamian mythology, the torch and the lightning (*tsullat* and *hanis*) are the heralds of the storm god" (Frymer-Kensky, page 46). So there seems to be some word-play here, which serves to contrast the God of Israel with competing gods of the time. Indeed, according to the Song of Deborah (Judges 5), Sisera's army was defeated by God through a storm.

The ancient Jewish gender category of *ay'lonit* refers to an assigned-female person who is infertile and develops masculine characteristics at puberty. I have to wonder if Deborah might have been an *ay'lonit*, since she took on such a prominent leadership role, there is no record of her children, and her marital status is unclear at best. Some say Sarah's infertility (see chapter 18) suggest that she was an *ay'lonit* (until God intervened). Rebekah, too, was a barren woman for many years and had some masculine characteristics. Unfortunately, discussion of *ay'lonit* in the Talmud tends to focus primarily on (in)fertility and *ay'lonit* is the least developed of the OtherWise gender identities in Judaism (Marsh).

The fiery Deborah does not change her sex or gender in the way we think of such things in the modern world. She continues to be recognized as a woman, even though she is not treated as one. She demonstrates the character of a man, and they treat her as such. Once again, we see that neither God nor Israel would be limited by rigid gender roles as assigned at birth. This gender non-conforming AFAB judge of Israel sits among the patriarchs, prophets, and kings, as a mother of Israel (Judges 5).

Judges 4–5 does not pretend to be a biography of Deborah. It leaves us with as many questions as it provides answers. Where did Deborah come from? How did she become a judge of Israel? What was her personal life like? What did people at that time think and feel about Deborah's gender? Deborah may not have been married and no children are identified for her. What we do know is that Deborah was a powerful woman who commanded powerful men, saved Israel, and was accepted and respected in a leadership role typically reserved for men of war. In the ancient world of men and unmen, this woman of fire and virility is our trans-masculine foremother.

♡

You are loved. When you are wandering on your own. When they do not know what to call you. When you seem to be the only one of your kind. You are loved.

Chapter 21
Resident Aliens and Feeling Different

You will regard the alien
who resides with you
as the native-born among you.
You are to love him as yourself,
for you were aliens
in the land of Egypt;
I am the LORD your God.

Leviticus 19:34
Christian Standard Bible

In the title theme from her book, *The Soul of the Stranger: Reading God and Torah from a Transgender Perspective*, Joy Ladin takes on the most fundamental binary of all of human experience—us versus them:

> But in the commandment not to oppress the stranger, God offers a... model for how communities should relate to members who are seen as too different to fit in, a model that rejects the idea that there is an unbridgeable gulf between those who are embraced as *us* and those who are... treated as *them*. "You shall not oppress a stranger, for you know the soul of the stranger, having yourselves been strangers in the land of Egypt" (Exodus 23:9). (Ladin, *The Soul of the Stranger*, page 140)

Some translations say, you know the "heart" or the "feelings" of the stranger. In other words, you can remember what it is like to be "that one" who is known primarily for being different and for not fitting in.

Ladin (following W. E. B. Du Bois) articulates the feelings of the stranger as

> lonely, awkward, and uncomfortable. ... Being seen as too different to understand... can also make us feel frustrated, overlooked, unappreciated, disregarded, deliberately spurned, despairing, and sometimes very angry. When we express those feelings, which tend to seem inexplicable to those around us, we become even more of a problem. (Ladin, *The Soul of the Stranger*, page 134)

Ladin argues that this experience of being a stranger is actually a universally human experience, insofar as each of us, no matter who or what we are, has had some experience in which we have felt "invisible and incomprehensible to those we live with and love, and felt rejected by words and actions that, to most members of the community, are simply routine" (Ladin, *The Soul of the Stranger*, page 137).

I have talked about the eunuch as foreigner and slave, but Ladin specifically explores the *ger*, the "stranger among us." This word *ger* is variously translated as "stranger" or "foreigner," but also as "resident alien." Ladin describes the nuance:

> The Israelites had lived in Egypt for many generations before they were enslaved, and in the wilderness they miss their old lives. Their nostalgia suggests that even when they were enslaved, the Israelites hadn't seen themselves as strangers; no matter how they were treated by the Egyptians, to them, Egypt was home. *That*—the experience of being treated as strangers in the society they felt to be their own—is what God orders the Israelites to recall in the commandment not to oppress the stranger. That is what *ger*... means: not someone who is a foreigner, with no permanent ties to Israelite society... but what U.S. immigration law calls a "resident alien"... a person who... lives in and is a part of Israelite community but is seen as too different to be considered one of us. (Ladin, *The Soul of the Stranger*, pages 141–142)

The *ger* is neither a tourist passing through nor a foreign ambassador. The *ger* is that stranger who has made a home among us—who, despite being from another place, has been woven into the fabric of our community.

Being a stranger is not only about nationality or immigration status. It is about whether we fully fit into or blend in among the community that we have claimed as our own:

> [T]he Hebrew word for converting to Judaism is *l'hitgayer*, which literally means "to make oneself a stranger": to become a Jew when you are not born a Jew is to identify yourself with a community in which you will always be considered a stranger. ... *ger* and *l'hitgayer*... refer to the long-term social situation of living in a community in which... no matter how long or how well we are known, we are always seen as too different to fully fit in or be considered one of us. (Ladin, *The Soul of the Stranger*, pages 143–144)

Becoming a stranger is about becoming a part of a community that is different from how or where you were born. It is about joining in while being yourself in a way that is still obviously different from those around you.

Ladin talks about the Passover laws in Exodus 12 as a "festival of binaries," designed to strengthen Israelite identity:

> [B]efore the first Passover, Israelites were identified not by religion but by ancestry: to be an Israelite (or "Hebrew"...) was to be a descendent of Abraham, Isaac, and Jacob. (Ladin, *The Soul of the Stranger*, page 114)

> These [Passover] laws are the Torah's equivalent of "Jewish Identity for Dummies." Many Jews find it hard to follow the complex system of Jewish law that grew out of centuries of rabbinic discussion. But all Jews, even children, can grasp binary distinctions like this. Food is either leavened or unleavened; leaven is either inside our houses or it isn't; people are either Jews, who have to celebrate Passover, or they are not. Passover is literally a festival of binaries, a festival we celebrate by changing our lives to fit Passover's either/or terms. (Ladin, *The Soul of the Stranger*, page 114)

In other words, Passover traditions are designed to accentuate difference—to help us identify those who belong and those who do not belong.

However, Ladin points out that both God and the rabbinic tradition also recognize that the binaries of Passover are easier to maintain in theory than in practice:

> At first, the law of the Passover offering is a model of binary simplicity: no foreigner... is permitted to eat the Passover sacrifice. But God immediately blurs the Israelite/non-Israelite binary by allowing two categories of non-Israelites to eat the sacrifice: circumcised non-Israelite slaves owned by Israelites, and "strangers" who have circumcised all the males in their households. Even here, in the laws of a festival that celebrates binary distinction... God considers it more important to include non-Israelites who identify with the community of Israel than to preserve the purity and simplicity of binary categories by excluding anyone who does not fit within them. (Ladin, *The Soul of the Stranger*, page 120)

In this major holiday that is about observing the boundaries of Jewish identity, God is also expanding the Jewish community to include slaves and strangers. Ladin argues that there are three approaches to dealing with human complexity that does not fit the binary: (1) force everyone to conform, (2) expand our categories, or (3) eliminate the binary altogether. In Passover, God chooses the more expansive approach, neither enforcing nor eliminating the binary.

Ladin reminds us that God, too, is a *ger*, a resident alien among us, incomprehensible and strange:

> God is not just a stranger in this or that community: God is the ultimate *ger*, a singular Presence who, as Judaism and other traditions which grow out of the Torah teach, dwells among human beings, sharing our lives, caring about our actions, knowing our sorrows and our struggles, but who can never fit in or be seen as one of us. ... Knowing the soul of the stranger is part of the spiritual discipline required for a community to make a place for God. (Ladin, *The Soul of the Stranger*, pages 146–147)

In other words, welcoming the stranger is not just charity work. It is a spiritual practice that draws us closer to God.

Thus, Ladin argues that God's command regarding the stranger is threefold. Through Passover, the Israelites were to "keep the memory of being strangers in Egypt alive and central to Israelite identity" (Ladin, *The Soul of the Stranger*, page 147). They were also to embrace the strangers among them, treat them as equals, and include them fully in community life (Numbers 15:15-16). Finally, they were to "identify with the experience of being the... stranger—the stranger who dwells among them, the strangers they are, the stranger who is God" (Ladin, *The Soul of the Stranger*, page 147).

Ladin assures us that God's commands require empathy, not necessarily understanding:

> This commandment does not presume or require that we know how any individual stranger feels. For that, we would have to get to know those we see as strangers as individuals, and God does not... command the Israelites to do that. Rather, God commands that we respond to seeing someone as a stranger by remembering the ways in which we too have felt or been seen as too strange to fit in with communities we consider our own. (Ladin, *The Soul of the Stranger*, page 145)

We do not need to feel compassion for or connection to those who are different from us because of some real or imagined common ground or similarity. We do not necessarily need to understand their experience at all. However, we are asked to remember that, however vast our differences may be, we have all shared this experience of being a resident alien, of being different, of standing out from the crowd as an "other."

Ladin's closing is beautiful ode to welcoming God as the ultimate resident alien (*ger*):

> [T]o welcome God into our communities is to welcome a stranger who will never assimilate, who will not go along to get along, who will not follow our rules, accept our judgments, embrace our values, affirm our doctrines, confirm our biases, or look and behave the way we expect—a stranger who may bless us or curse us, who is responsible for all the good and all the evil that befalls us, who takes without asking and gives without explanation. To love God, we must learn to love someone who will always

> be a stranger. To serve God, we must serve the needs of a stranger. To grow close to God, we must become intimate with a stranger. To open ourselves to God, we must open ourselves to a stranger. To make a place for the God who dwells invisibly and incomprehensibly among us—to show that God belongs with us, and that we belong to God—we must know, and build our lives and communities around knowing, the soul of the stranger. (Ladin, *The Soul of the Stranger*, page 147)

Ladin's teaching around welcoming the stranger speaks deeply to the predicament of those of us who regularly find ourselves to be strange, weird, queer, or OtherWise alien in our families and communities. Being OtherWise resident aliens ourselves means that we are kindred spirits with both God and the Israelites. Rather than emphasizing and enforcing the "us vs. them" binary, Jewish tradition teaches about the sacred power of hospitality and enduring relationship despite our differences. We can feel as strange as a resident alien, but that feeling can also bring us closer to God. We may actually be as queer as a three-dollar bill, but still God commands that there must be space for such strangers to be embraced as a part of God's covenant community. Indeed, this teaching is also a challenge to ensure that our own OtherWise communities are as flexible and fluid as those of the Israelites when *we* encounter the stranger among us.

May we claim this lineage of Abraham and Isaac, of Jacob and Joseph, of Deborah and Rebekah, of foreigners and strangers. May we make space for our shared humanity in the midst of all the binaries that we face. May we all know God as we have known the stranger among us and the stranger who is us.

♡

You are loved. When you feel like the problem. When you feel like a resident alien. When you are welcomed for all of who you are. You are loved.

SECTION SIX
OtherWise Christian Traditions

Chapter 22
Letters of Liberation

Galatians 3:28

There is no longer
Jew or Gentile,
slave or free,
male and female.
For you are all
one in Christ Jesus.

Galatians 3:28
New Living Translation

The Apostle Paul is a very influential figure in Christian tradition. In Galatians 3:28, 1 Corinthians 12:13 and Colossians 3:11, he variously writes about how unity in Christ Jesus breaks down barriers such as Jew and Gentile, slave or free. Scholars suggest that these binary formulations may reflect an early baptismal formula that preceded Paul.

A plain reading of the Galatians text specifically suggests that the categories "male and female" have been abolished in favor of a new Christian unity. However, many Christians have argued that such a reading is too literal. Pat Conover concedes, "Galatians 3:28 makes no sense as scientific observation" (Conover, page 226). In other passages, Paul seems to argue in favor of the gender conventions of his time and culture (see appendix A for some examples).

Yet, I noted in chapter 17 that some early Christians did adopt an abolitionist perspective on gender. They advocated for abstinence not only from sex and gender distinctions, but from gender roles and family obligations entirely. Clearly, some kind of significant egalitarian impulse was sustained beyond the ministry of Jesus.

Justin Tanis offers a more nuanced option for interpreting this verse, somewhere between erasing and enforcing these categories:

> Paul is not simply ignoring or erasing differences here, but rather altering the way in which we relate to those differences. Unity in Christ requires us to treat people as equals without prejudice. (Tanis, pages 81–82)

This "altering" approach also resonates with Joy Ladin's argument about adding nuance to the Israelite/non-Israelite binary in order to be more inclusive (see chapter 21). The gender binary does not disappear entirely in Christ, but God does have higher priority concerns, such as relationship and connection.

The first few decades after Jesus lived were a tumultuous time as news of the resurrection spread and the church grew. While Jesus had a significant following in his earthly life, he had not been about the business of shaping Christian institutional life nor even creating a written record of his teachings. So there were many questions (and opportunities for conflict) left for the Apostles and the new Christian communities as they explored together what it meant to live "in Christ Jesus." The numerous letters attributed to Paul are some of the earliest church writings, as the traveling evangelist corresponded with emergent communities in those formative years. You might think of the Pauline letters as text messages from a mentor in the faith—only in a time before cell phones, emails, printers, and copy machines. The early Christians would copy by hand and rewrite, read and reread these letters to keep as a sacred record and for future reference.

Galatians (with 1 and 2 Thessalonians and 1 Corinthians) is believed to be one of the earliest remaining documents available from that time when Christians were grappling with key questions of community formation. Scholars agree that Paul's letter to the Galatians (approximately 20 years after Jesus) was written even before the book of Acts (approximately 80–90 CE) and the four Gospels (in the period 66–110 CE). Baptism had been established as a practice even before Jesus, when John the Baptist was preaching a baptism of repentance in the wilderness. However, this practice became even more significant for Jesus and his followers, as baptism was (and is) used to mark the beginning of a Christian's journey in Christ.

In chapter 15, I talked about the Ethiopian eunuch traveler (Acts 8) in the wilderness who asked, "What is to prevent me from being baptized?" Some scholars believe that question is also part of an early baptismal formula. Acts 8 provides its own answer to the question as the traveler is immediately baptized—without concern for his class, nationality, OtherWise gender experience, or religious background. The categories that made the Acts 8 traveler remarkable are the same categories reflected here in Galatians 3:28.

If we connect the two baptismal formulas, we find an even more explicit answer to the traveler's question:

> For in Christ Jesus you are all sons of God through faith. For all of you who were baptized into Christ have clothed yourselves with Christ. There is neither Jew nor Greek, there is neither slave nor free, there is neither

> male nor female—for all of you are one in Christ Jesus. And if you belong to Christ, then you are Abraham's descendants, heirs according to the promise. (Galatians 3:26–29 New English Translation)

Paul argues that none of these worldly distinctions matter when it comes to baptism and beginning a new life in Christ.

In this section, the phrase "sons of God" can also be translated more inclusively as "children" or "descendents" of God, but it is a masculine part of speech. Thinking more specifically about the construction of gender in ancient times, it matters that the binary-busting proclamation of Galatians 3:28 comes in the context of these verses about sons and heirs. We all become sons and heirs through baptism. Not only men, but also unmen (see chapter 4), for there is no longer "male and female." Women become sons and heirs. Eunuchs become sons and heirs. Even children become sons and heirs in Christ Jesus.

While Deborah's virtue (*virtus*) (see chapter 20) allowed her to "move up the ladder toward manly perfection" (DeFranza, page 114), baptism moves each of us toward perfection, not by any virtue of our own, but because of Christ Jesus. This is also the radical gender-full equality that Jesus evoked when he aligned himself with eunuchs (and children) in Matthew 19 (see chapter 14). The promise that was once only for descendents of Abraham, Isaac, and Jacob (see chapter 18) also became a promise for slaves and resident aliens (see chapter 21), eunuchs and foreigners (see chapter 13) in Israel. By virtue of this new baptism in Christ, that promise is articulated in Galatians as being for both men and women, for Israelites and non-Israelites.

Virginia Mollenkott and others before her note the lack of parallelism between "Jew *or* Gentile," "slave *or* free," and "male *and* female" (which is not retained in all translations) and wonder if there is any meaning to be found in the shift (Mollenkott, 2007 edition, page xii). The "male and female" phrase echoes the creation story in Genesis 1:27 (see chapter 6), where "God created them male and female." Here, Paul seems to be evoking that first family, first relationship, as he speaks about expanding God's community with additional sons and heirs of Abraham. This echo reminds us of creation and the idea that "male and female" is a *merism* that evokes all gender differentiation, not just the two binary options (see chapter 6).

The creation allusion also aligns with Paul's proclamation of a "new creation" in Christ (for instance, 2 Corinthians 5:17). Even if we were to take Genesis 1:27 as an original proclamation of two mutually exclusive genders purposed around complementarian reproduction (see chapters 6 and 7), Paul proclaims a transformation in Christ where "male and female" are somehow no more. Is this an argument about procreative sexuality being unecessary in this new creation? Alternately, if we read "male and female" as a *merism*, then perhaps Paul is proclaiming that all manner of sex and gender differentiation will be transformed in this new creation.

Following Joy Ladin's examination of Passover law (see chapter 21), it is useful specifically to consider Paul's relationship to the binaries in this list—is he enforcing, eliminating, or blurring the boundaries? While a comprehensive critique of Paul's theology is beyond the scope of this book, scholars have made each of these arguments about him. In light of the total arc of tradition (both Jewish and Christian), I believe that Paul is advocating for the significance of these categories to be diminished in favor of growing God's OtherWise family. Ladin has shown us that this tendency already exists in the Hebrew text and Jewish tradition. Meanwhile, Jesus is forever associating with women in unorthodox ways, which also demonstrates that this shift was a part of his ministry. It is not that our differences become meaningless, but that our relationships with one another are contextualized when they happen within God's eclectic family of strangers.

Paul was most certainly a product of his time and culture, but he was also on the cutting edge of the emergent and evolving Jesus movement. Women (and other unmen) could become "spiritual males" in Christ, without necessarily being considered categorically equal. Celibacy was becoming an admirable alternative to (heterosexual) marriage. Masculinity was being redefined in response to the teachings of Jesus. Creation itself was being born again in light of Christ's resurrection. Ultimately, the diversity of interpretations of Paul's statement in Galatians 3:28 is part of what makes the text so powerful.

In short, this Galatians 3:28 text is a source of hope and assurance for OtherWise-gendered Christians. Justin Tanis puts it this way from his own experience,

> Galatians 3:28 signified for me a radical shift in my understanding of what it meant to be in Christ; I was no longer bound to the divisions of gender, or to the roles our society assigns to women, but was set free by Christ. This verse was part of what enabled me to identify as a Christian and to claim for myself my Christian heritage, because I could see this new world opening up before me, a world in which gender was not the ultimate dividing force in my life. (Tanis, page 80)

May our freedom in Christ provide us with confidence that enables us to resist the many different structures of supremacy that dominate this world. May our liberation draw us nearer to one another and to God. May God's OtherWise family continue to expand and to embrace all those who may be burdened by the boundaries and binaries of this world.

♡

You are loved. When you are asking tough questions. When you wonder where you fit in. When you are claiming the promises of your ancestors. You are loved.

Chapter 23
Gospel-Style Resistance

I have come
that they may have life,
and that they may have it
more abundantly.

John 10:10b NKJV

At this point, I have spent 22 chapters describing just how common and acceptable OtherWise-gendered experiences have been in the world and, specifically, in Jewish and Christian traditions. Yet, we do not live in a world where these understandings are prominent. My hope is that this book will have some role in changing that dynamic, but I am sure that there will remain significant resistance to OtherWise-gendered people by those with power in both church and society. With that in mind, I want to talk about some other Christian texts that are not so specifically about gender but, rather, about being a part of a resistance movement.

Refugees and Asylum Seekers

In the birth narratives in Matthew, we find an entire class of children hunted down and slaughtered because of their gender (Matthew 2:16–18). Someone powerful decided that these children were a threat and decided to have them destroyed. I wish this analogy would finally grow old and outdated, but we live in a world where children continue to be used as pawns in political games without regard for their safety or well-being. It happens over religion; it happens over national borders; and it happens over gender. In Matthew, Jesus and his family became refugees in Egypt (Matthew 2:13–15, 19–23) because of just this kind of cruelty from those in positions of power.

OtherWise-gendered people are at risk in a variety of ways in many parts of the world, including the United States. The Matthew text shows that there are times when being a part of the resistance means leaving town to find safety. Sometimes resistance means hiding in some safe way so you can survive to fight another day. While visibility and stubborn persistence have their place, they are not the only honorable and faithful ways to be a part of the resistance. The threats on our lives can be very real. When God calls you into the wilderness, you will know it in your bones, but at some other times the best wisdom is to find refuge.

Protest and Disruption

In John 2:13–17, Jesus cleared the Temple in a rage, wielding a whip and overturning tables. There must have been oxen and sheep roaming free in the temple, money strewn on the ground, mingled with animal droppings in that sacred space. The scripture says, he made the whip of cords himself, so this was a deliberate premeditated act on Jesus' part to shake things up. It took time and forethought to create such a planned disturbance.

This is not the Jesus that I learned about in white, professional-class mainline Protestant churches growing up! This Jesus comes into our comfortable lives and jars our expectations. He puts the sacred places of our lives into chaos. In other words, Jesus rocks our world. We go to church and pay our taxes. We try to do the right thing and genuinely pray with deep concern for the ways the world around us seems to be falling apart. Yet, Jesus comes into these decent and well-intentioned Temples of our lives and overturns our tables with rage and diligence.

We point our fingers at those who disrupt, but, all too often, policies and players are deployed on a collision course long before things become volatile in an obvious way. What warning signs do we ignore along the way? The text suggests that Jesus may have been hanging around the Temple for some time weaving this whip. Maybe there were conversations about his concerns. Maybe other religious leaders thought he was "too idealistic," that he was "asking for too much." Maybe this traveling teacher, unmarried eunuch, was just not respectable enough to be taken seriously. Which voices are expendable, and who do we write off as unreliable or unreputable sources? What disparities do we fail to notice in those sacred places, the innermost sanctums of our lives? What conflicts, trials, and tribulations might turn out differently, if we did not pass these opportunities by?

There is a place for active, disruptive protest in the Christian life. It is not the entire ministry of Jesus, but it is a part of his ministry. He shows us a righteous anger that interrupts systems that exploit others. He did this as Passover was approaching, so even major holidays (religious or secular) should not be exempt, if they are furthering the cause of empire and exploitation instead of nourishing healing and transformation.

Privilege and Access

We usually talk about the disciples of Jesus being fisherfolk, working class guys with dirty boats and dirty fingernails, whose livelihood is at the mercy of the elements. We talk about the prostitutes and tax collectors, outcasts who are grudgingly tolerated at the margins of acceptable society and often at the mercy of an impulsive mob. We talk about the lepers and paraplegics, the sick and the blind, people who find themselves vulnerable to any able-bodied person who chooses to take advantage. We usually talk about people who come to Jesus in search of restoration, dignity, and hope, and Jesus reaches out to welcome, to heal, and to empower them.

Meanwhile, Nicodemus was a devout, well-intentioned man of privilege and means, right with God, respected in the community. He was different from most of the people we see following Jesus. Nicodemus was at the mercy of no one and in control of his own life with no concern about where his next meal would come from. He was a professional-class Jew, who worked in the Temple, a scholar and teacher, a community and religious leader. Nick never did drop everything to follow Jesus, not in the way the rest of the disciples appeared to, joining the throng in search of miracles or Armageddon, leaving jobs and family behind. Nick remained a devout, well-intentioned man of privilege and means, who continued to go to Temple and sit on the high council, just as he did before Jesus came.

We meet Nicodemus in John 3:1–21, right after Jesus cleared the Temple in protest. Nicodemus is frequently referred to as the "one who comes to Jesus at night," and he is often assumed to be a coward because of it. Perhaps he was a self-serving bureaucrat who sought out Jesus in secret, when no one else would see. We attribute a shrewd political mind, unwilling to commit fully to "the movement." We question his character. What if Nick has been misunderstood? What if Nick's arrival by night shows vulnerability and openness? Maybe Nick was in the Temple when Jesus came with his handmade whip—and maybe Jesus rocked his world. Maybe Nick laid awake that night, unable to sleep. Maybe his mind was churning over the events of the day. Maybe he was preoccupied with this prophet (or renegade) who made chaos out of Nick's well-meaning life. Maybe Nick was trying to make sense out the way Jesus spoke of the destruction of Nick's beloved Temple—the destruction of Nick's very best intentions.

I read the midnight visit between Jesus and Nicodemus a bit differently than most. Jesus tells Nicodemus, "Do not be surprised because I tell you that you must all be born again" (John 3:7). This story is often read as a teaching about salvation, but it is also a story about the way Jesus invites Nicodemus to start over with a new set of priorities. Jesus challenges

Nick to do a better job of receiving difficult and unexpected testimonies. "We speak of what we know, and we testify to what we have seen, but still you people do not accept our testimony" (John 3:11 NIV). Jesus tells Nick to begin again like a little child—vulnerable and open to new insights.

In other words, Jesus confronted Nicodemus in his privilege. Jesus challenged Nick to let go of being respectable and right. Jesus shook the foundations of Nick's world with his Temple action and that night he challenged Nick to venture out of the safety and security of the structures that have nurtured him. The text does not tell us about how Nick took this correction, and there is no "went away sad" moment (like the rich man in Matthew 19:22, Mark 10:22, and Luke 18:23). The Gospel just moves on until we meet Nick again.

If Nick's midnight arrival did represent some political expediency, it still took a lot of guts for a leader from that same Temple to come to this Jesus of the overturned tables to listen—for Nick to put himself in relationship with someone who had already challenged the foundations of his life in a very public way. That takes courage and character, character that shows up several chapters later when we find Nicodemus confronting his peers on the High Council about their rabid pursuit of Jesus arrest (John 7:50–52). Nick put his own privilege on the line to speak truth to power.

Later, when Jesus had been crucified and all the other disciples fled in fear and despair—in those terrible three days when "the movement" had been utterly destroyed—Nick joined with Joseph of Arimathea to bury Jesus' body (John 19:38–40). This was a provocative action that could have dramatic repercussions on Nick's livelihood and life among his peers. This good Jew contributed over 100 pounds of myrrh and aloe to honor the unclean body of an outcast. In that moment, when there was nothing to be gained, no crowd of disciples to join with, no wandering prophet to follow, Nick risked his reputation again to honor a condemned criminal, convicted blasphemer, and political renegade. He held close the body of a man who had been cut off from his own people. Without denying or running from his identity as a man of privilege and means, Nicodemus put it all on thc line.

Nicodemus is a lot like so many Christian folk who feel right with God and respected in the community. Many of us are professional-class people, scholars and teachers, community and religious leaders with a lot to lose. Jesus has come into our lives and we go back to work to sit on committees and do our jobs. If we understand that Nick was a lot like us, then this story is also a challenge that demands something of us: to seek out the Spirit in unexpected and disturbing places and to set aside concern for our power and privilege if it prevents us from fully receiving the witness of that Spirit.

Jesus says you may not find me in your Temple—in the decent and orderly places of your lives, no matter how sacred. Instead, look to the places that trouble you. You may find me in the dirty gutters and back alleyways surviving on scraps of food from trash cans, or in prisons and mental institutions challenging your definitions of propriety. You may find me in after-hours nightclubs reaching and longing for life. You may find me in the deep dark places of your soul where there is struggle and turmoil, isolation and pain. I will not ask your forgiveness, when I leave you feeling disturbed. I will rock your world. Get used to it.

The Gospel is as disturbing as it is liberating. Nicodemus and Jesus both challenge us to evaluate comfortable middle-class priorities. Jesus and Nicodemus show us that we can resist the powers of this world—powers that will bamboozle us into thinking that acting like white, professional-class men and women is the only respectable way to be in God's family. We need to be ready to let go of our privilege and access whenever it gets in the way of doing the right thing.

Grief and Joy

The Beatitudes (in Matthew 5 and Luke 6) remind us that resistance can be hard: mourning and hunger, persecution and thirst. Jesus does not tell us that he will make these things disappear. He does not tell us it will be easy. He only tells us that we will be blessed. Resistance to the powers and principalities of this world will be difficult. The empire is alive and well. There is no need to pretend otherwise. We can take time to grieve our losses. We can invest in sorting through our trauma and tending to our fears and insecurities. We can bring one another food and water, encouragement and uplift, in the midst of our struggles.

The beatitudes also tell us to "rejoice and be glad" (Matthew 5:12a). Thanks to an unpublished sermon from Patricia Pearce, I do not believe that this means we should be glad about our suffering but rather that, in order to keep resisting, we need to take time to find and nourish our joy. We should celebrate small victories, spend time with loved ones, find reasons to laugh, and enjoy doing what we love (whether that is going for a walk in nature, making art, playing video games, or whatever!). The world can be a terrible place, and we will not survive it unless we take the time to replenish our spirits.

Boundaries and Letting Go

In Matthew 18:10–14 (NIV), Jesus offered the parable of the lost sheep. He said, "If a man owns a hundred sheep, and one of them wanders away, will he not leave the 99 on the hills and go to look for the one that wandered off?" Yet, in John 17:12 (NIV), Jesus showed no apparent concern for Judas having been lost. He says, "While I was with them, I protected them and kept them safe by that name you gave me. None has been lost except the one doomed to destruction so that Scripture would be fulfilled."

Of course, I know that Judas was the ultimate fall guy, "The one who betrayed our Lord." If there is anybody we, as Christians, should love to hate, it would have to be Judas. No wonder neither the Gospel writers or most biblical commentaries I have consulted seem to give much thought to the loss of Judas. Yet, it is really kind of disturbing to find that Jesus contradicted his own teaching in this way.

In my reading of these two texts, Judas was the ultimate lost sheep. He was one of the good guys, one of Jesus' partners in ministry. Judas was an insider, one of the 12 guys in the middle of the action. He was not just any old sheep—he was one of the favorite sheep and he got lost. Here, the Good Shepherd himself lost a sheep, justified it with the Bible, and then went on with his business. The reality of the relationship between Jesus and Judas contradicted Jesus' own teaching. Sure. Judas deserved to pay for his betrayal of Christ, but don't we all? What about the lost sheep? The lost coin? The prodigal son? What about going the extra mile? What about our pursuit of reconciliation and forgiveness? What about our walking the talk? And practicing what we preach? How could Jesus give up on Judas?

Well, how do we feel when someone close to us hurts us badly? When we feel we have been betrayed? When we no longer feel we can trust someone we once counted on? What are we supposed to do when a close relationship is in painful conflict and only seems to be getting worse? Maybe you have wrestled with a painful relationship where it hurts just to think about what might have gone wrong—where you or someone you love has finally had to walk away. I do, and there are voices in my own head that call me stubborn, resentful, uncharitable, and unforgiving, even unChristian. It challenges my idealism.

Sometimes, we do have to let go. Eventually, I realized that I am only human. It is not only that I cannot fix everything, it is also that it is not my responsibility to fix everything. As much as I would like to believe differently, I do have limitations. I get confused and emotional. I misunderstand things. I get hurt and defensive. I can only handle so much—as hard as that is to admit. Because I am human, I can only take so much.

Maybe that is what Jesus meant when he conceded his relationship with Judas in prayer. Maybe he simply meant that he was finally at peace giving it up to God. Maybe, in that moment, Jesus, in his full humanity, was conceding his own limitations. Perhaps, citing scripture and God's greater wisdom was simply his way of letting go of a failed relationship with Judas—letting Judas go into the mystery of a loving God. If Jesus had to let go into this mystery, so much more should we.

Sometimes my best just is not good enough—but it is, after all, all that I have to give. Since I am human, I have to trust God to make up the difference. In this world, there will be irreconcilable differences, insurmountable obstacles, and deep losses that affect us as humans struggling under empire. We will not find peace just because we tried hard enough or wanted it badly enough. Faithfulness does not always mean overcoming. We will only find peace when we stop trying to be God long enough to let go and let God really work in the midst of our brokenness.

Disclosure and Intimacy

The transfiguration of Jesus appears in all three synoptic Gospels (Matthew 17:1–9; Mark 9:2–9; Luke 9:28–36). In each account, Jesus goes up onto a mountain with several disciples. While there, the disciples see Jesus transfigured and in relationship with revered Jewish leaders, Moses and Elijah. Jesus was seen in all of his glory and splendor, dazzling with light. This was truly a "mountain top" experience. Why not build a shrine or a retreat center at this sacred spot? Indeed, upon seeing Jesus like this, the disciples wanted to make camp and offered to build three shelters—one each for Jesus, Moses, and Elijah. However, this was not to be. The moment passed and, on the way back down the mountain, Jesus admonished the disciples not to tell anyone about it.

In every life, there will be moments of inspiration and clarity, sometimes even "mountain top" experiences. Here, Jesus disclosed his true identity to his closest friends in a moment of intimacy and vulnerability. It is no small thing to find a few friends with whom we can unpack both our biggest dreams and our heaviest baggage. Sometimes, we do not even fully understand ourselves until we have had that experience of being really seen and understood by a loved one. These are precious moments that transform everyone involved.

Indeed, those disciples would never see their friend, Jesus, in the same way again. They were supportive and excited about the revelation they had been given. Yet, Jesus swears them to secrecy. Jesus trusted these friends with game-changing information that could have put Jesus at risk. In that disclosure, he gave over some power and control to those who were closest to him, not knowing for sure how they would respond. Maybe he was not ready for others to know; maybe he had his own timeline and priorities for sharing the news; or maybe he just needed to test the waters before he went "all in."

Like Jesus, it can also be healing and empowering for us to share our most authentic self with close confidantes. It can be risky; it may not always go well; and we may encounter rejection or betrayal. Not everyone is worthy of our trust. We may gain affirmation or valuable feedback. The sense of rest and repair that can come in the loving care of our friends is a profoundly important resource for those of us who spend our lives resisting the powers that be. It is also a natural impulse to want to settle in to such a time of retreat, to make camp, build a shelter, and stay a while. Yet, Jesus calls us back down the mountain to engage again with the world. Not every intimacy needs to be shared with the world. We need some private times when we can withdraw and repair, experiment and prepare. We need both.

Gospel-Style Resistance

As OtherWise-gendered folk, we have been given a truth that may seem improbable, illogical, or outrageous. We live our lives in ways that so many others cannot even imagine. Our testimonies may be laughable, strange, or queer, much like our ancestors before us. We may even be misunderstood in ways that undermine our respectable reputations. Yet, with God's help, our witness has been sustained through the centuries against all odds. We continue to resist today—and Christ, the human one, who overturns tables, is with us, in laughter and in tears, showing the way forward.

♡

You are loved. When you take refuge. When you have to let go. When you make your position known, come what may. When you resist. You are loved.

Chapter 24
Otherwise Disciples and OtherWise Jesus

She had a sister called Mary,
who sat at the Lord's feet
listening to what he said.
But Martha was distracted
by all the preparations
that had to be made.

Luke 10:39–40a NIV

[Jesus] *replied,*
"As you enter the city,
a man carrying a jar of water
will meet you.
Follow him
to the house
that he enters."

Luke 22:10 NIV

Throughout the Gospels, Jesus disrupts a variety of cultural conventions, including the way men and women typically interacted. In many ways, Jesus himself is the most OtherWise character in the Greek scriptures. Yet, there are two OtherWise characters who do stand out, both brought to light by Peterson Toscano in his play, *Transfigurations: Transgressing Gender in the Bible.*

Mary and Martha

Luke 10:38–42

In Luke 10:38–42, we find Jesus visiting the home of Martha in Bethany. Already, this is a curious scenario to see a woman as apparent head of household. She must have been a fairly wealthy woman in order to have a home large enough to host Jesus and his followers. In a different story in the Gospel of John, Martha is quite forward, going so far as to reprimand Jesus for not coming to their aid quickly enough (John 11:21)! She apparently lives with her sister while their brother, Lazarus, lives nearby (John 11:1–2). None of this fits with what was customary behavior for women of the time.

Back in the Luke 10 scene, Martha was busy with household concerns. Presumably, their house was full of people who were traveling with Jesus, and Martha was fulfilling important hospitality obligations, as was expected in their culture. Meanwhile, Martha's sister, Mary, was sitting at the feet of Jesus listening to his teachings as a disciple. As the scene plays out, Martha asks Jesus to reprimand Mary for not helping her out with the hospitality concerns, but Jesus sides with Mary. In this exchange, Martha seems to be taking the feminine role, despite being head of household, while Mary is engaging in religious study, which was commonly reserved for men. While not as extreme as the gender-transgressive Deborah (see chapter 20), Mary and Martha are both acting in ways that were unusual for women. Yet, Jesus is particularly fond of them (John 11:5).

There are several Marys in the Gospels, including Mary of Bethany, Mary Magdalene, Mary the mother of Jesus, and at least one unnamed woman who is often believed to be a Mary. The Gospels sometimes make a point of saying "Mary the mother of Jesus" or "Mary who was the sister of Lazarus," but other times the text is not clear. As the tradition evolved, the many Marys were sometimes combined into a composite "Mary" disciple (at least in part because in 1591 CE, Pope Gregory the Great said they were all the same person!). Yet, Matthew 28:1 tells us that "Mary Magdalene and the other Mary" went to the tomb, so we know that there was definitely more than one. While Mary of Bethany was portrayed as a part of this beloved sibling group, Mary Magdalene appears frequently in the Gospels and is sometimes called the "apostle to the apostles" because of her role in proclaiming the resurrection.

Mary Magdalene is a regular character in several non-canonical (gnostic) Gospels, but the closing scene of the Gospel of Thomas is quite relevant here, and it just says "Mary." Scholars disagree about whether the Gospel of Thomas was an early text (approx 40 CE) or a late one (approx 140 CE). Either way, it did not make it into the Bible. In its closing scene, similar to Martha, Simon Peter wants to send Mary away because she is a woman. Jesus responds by saying he will make Mary into a man:

> Look, I will lead her that I may make her male, in order that she too may become a living spirit resembling you males. For every woman who makes herself male will enter into the kingdom of heaven. (Gospel of Thomas, saying 114b, Blatz translation)

The church does not take the Gospel of Thomas as an authentic or authoritative Gospel—and this saying also holds a great deal of misogyny. However, this non-canonical tradition confirms that Jesus had developed quite a reputation for enabling Mary (one or more of them!) to exceed her assigned-gender role(s). Like Paul, proclaiming that we all become sons and heirs in Christ (see chapter 22), the Thomas text demonstrates the way Jesus was believed to help women, like Mary, climb the "ladder of perfection" to become men (see chapters 4 and 20).

Thinking of Mary (of Bethany) as literally or figuratively becoming male, a number of possibilities emerge. How does it change the way that we think of Martha and Mary living together, if Mary was becoming a man? Were they biological siblings or just "women living together as sisters"? If Jesus was teaching Mary to be a man, then how might that change their relationship over time? Any way you look at it, Mary was an OtherWise-gendered disciple, who was well known for casting aside the gender roles she was assigned at birth—and, clearly, Martha was not the only one talking about it.

The Water Carrier

Mark 14:13–15; Luke 22:8–13; Matthew 26:17–19

Our second OtherWise disciple appears in all three of the synoptic Gospels (Mark 14:13–15; Luke 22:8–13; and obliquely in Matthew 26:17–19). Jesus and the disciples needed a place to have the Passover meal. Jesus sent Peter and John ahead to find a "man carrying a jug of water." In Matthew, they are sent to find "a certain man" which raises the question, "Which one?" However, in that time, carrying water was the task of unmen—women, children, and slaves. So, this was not just any man. This was a certain kind of man, an unusual kind of man, the kind of man who would be carrying a jar of water.

The Greek for "man" in Mark and Luke is *anthropos*, which in no way suggests a child, eunuch, or slave (though it can sometimes function like "human"). Some scholars argue that this "certain" man must have been an Essene. As such, he would have been unmarried and celibate, living in a religious community with other men. According to this theory, the man with the jug of water was a figurative, if not literal, eunuch. Indeed, the Essene communities were Jewish precursors to the Christian monks who would later be called "eunuchs for the kingdom" (see chapters 14 and 17). The Essenes followed a different calendar, so this could also explain why they might have an empty room available during such an important holiday.

Toscano playfully imagined a different scenario, one where a person assigned-male-at-birth (AMAB) has decided to transition to a new identity. He constructs an awkward coming-out scene between this new-in-transition transgender woman and her family. The disclosure does not end well, and everyone leaves in a huff. Toscano then portrays this woman (who was still presenting as male, except for the jar of water) encountering the disciples and offering the family's room, which is now empty. While the playwright is generally projecting modern experiences back in time for the sake of good theater, it is not a completely impossible scenario. A family member deciding to become a eunuch and/or join the Essenes could cause a similar kerfuffle.

Genetic Jesus

In chapter 14, I explored how Jesus referred to eunuchs in his teachings. A more speculative treatment asks just how OtherWise was Jesus? It is likely that Jesus was called a eunuch (at least as a slur), because he was an unmarried adult male. Rather than deny that identity, Jesus aligned himself closely with eunuchs in Matthew 19:11–12. Nonetheless, many have speculated about Jesus, including those who suggest he had a gay lover, the beloved disciple (perhaps Lazarus). Others believe that the intimate relationship between Jesus and Mary Magdalene was consummated with marriage, sexual intercourse, and a child. In each case, speculation extrapolates from dynamics that are embedded in the text.

Similarly, Edward Kessel published a thesis in 1983 extrapolating from the virgin birth of Jesus. Kessel notes scientific evidence of parthenogenesis, which can be thought of as asexual reproduction. In parthenogenetic reproduction, there is no male sperm contribution to fertilize the egg. Scientists, such as H. Spurway, have argued that virgin birth is "probable among humans" (cited in Kessel), though they admit that parthenogenetic birth is not likely to be reported, due to confirmation bias. In other words, no one believes a woman who claims to have become pregnant without sexual intercourse.

Jesus was circumcised as a child (Luke 2:21) and may have died naked on the cross. So it is very likely that his genitalia appeared to be that of a typical male. Jesus should have had XX or XO chromosomes, if he was conceived parthenogenetically. There was no one involved to contribute the (typically) male Y chromosome. Nonetheless, Kessel considers the possibility that Mary, the mother of Jesus (neither Mary of Bethany, nor Mary Magdalene), may have had an intersex genetic variation that could provide a Y chromosome to the parthenogenetic process.

Putting the mother of Jesus aside, there are at least two intersex conditions that could account for the genetically female, physiologically male result. Mosaic XY/XO xy-Turners Syndrome frequently results in typically male infant genitals but does not lead to a typical male puberty. Similarly, de la Chapelle/XX Male Sex Reversal Syndrome frequently results in typically male infant genitals with infertility and sometimes small testes and breast development at puberty. In either case, Jesus may have had a more effeminate puberty than we would typically assume, which could have further contributed to his being called a eunuch. While most readers assume that Jesus identified himself as a "eunuch for the sake of the kingdom of heaven" in Matthew 19:12, this biological analysis suggests that he might also have been a "eunuch from birth."

Meanwhile, God works in mysterious ways. Some have argued that Mother Mary was a virgin, as in maiden, but not sexually chaste. Others note that God could have miraculously thrown in a Y chromosome, if God felt like it! Who are we to place limits on the Divine One? In the end, we are always making assumptions and drawing conclusions based on a religious text, not a proper historical or scientific document. Even so, from a theological point of view, a parthenogenetic intersex Jesus could be considered the perfect image of God, "male and female." As Kessel puts it, "Christ was a man. Christ was also a woman" (Kessel).

OtherWise Jesus

Virginia Mollenkott goes beyond specific individual examples to suggest that the very metaphors of Christian discipleship point to cross-gender realities in the kingdom of God (Mollenkott, 2007 edition, pages 126–128). In chapter 22, I touched on the way baptism in Christ makes all Christians sons and heirs. Scripture (for example, Roman 4:1 and 1 Corinthians 6:6) also refers to members of the Christian community as *adelphos*, which means brother. This word, *adelphos*, is increasingly translated as "brothers and sisters," in order to be more inclusive. However, the Greek is masculine, even though Paul is clearly referring to churches (for example, in Rome or Corinth) that included women. Further, these gender assignments occur alongside the metaphors that make women disciples a part of the body of Christ, which is assumed to be male like Jesus. Might that mean that all Christian women are masculine or virile women? Does Christian discipleship make a woman, like Mary of Bethany, transgender?

Meanwhile, both Jesus and Paul use the marriage metaphor. Jesus calls himself the bridegroom (Matthew 9:15; John 3:29), while Paul refers to the church as bride (Ephesians 5:25–27; 2 Corinthians 11:2). These references are similar to the way that Hebrew scripture refers to the nation of Israel as a wife or bride (Isaiah 54:4–8; Jeremiah 31:31–33; Hosea 2:14–20) or even daughter (Micah 4:8; Jeremiah 14:17). Insofar as men are a part of the church (or the nation of Israel), they are metaphorically taking on a feminine form through Christian discipleship. Might that mean that all Christian men are also effeminate men? Does Christian discipleship make men into not just eunuchs, but women betrothed to Christ Jesus?

Obviously, all of this imagery is metaphorical, not literal, though even that distinction reflects a modern worldview that prioritizes biology as the determining factor in sex assignment. In any case, we do not need Jesus to be genetically or physiologically intersex in order for gender references to be quite complicated in the body of Christ (which is the Christian church). Christian men are part of the (female) bride of Christ. Christian women are brothers, sons, and part of the (presumably male) body of Christ. We are the image of Christ (Romans 8:29); Christ is the image of God (Colossians 1:15); and God's image was created "male and female" (Genesis 1:27).

There are other gender-bending metaphors, too. Jesus was considered the Word (*Logos* in John 1), which is a masculine parallel to the feminine Wisdom (*Sophia* in Proverbs 8). Jesus even identified himself with Wisdom in Matthew 11:19. In John 16:21–22, Jesus talks about a woman's giving birth because her "time has come." In the very next verse, Jesus says "the hour has come" (John 17:1) about himself. While Paul's gender is not our focus, he, too, identifies as a woman, that is, as a mother giving birth in Galatians 4:19. Considering Jesus at least figuratively intersex is one of the only ways to make sense out of this constellation of metaphors—though we might also look again to Paul's proclamation that, in Christ, there is no "male and female" (see chapter 22).

OtherWise Discipleship

God, Jesus, and even Paul defy the male/female binary. Like Sarah's laughable non-binary status as both an old woman and a new mother (see chapter 18), these key characters in Christian tradition defy the idea of two mutually exclusive genders as defined by biology at birth. We, too, as children and siblings, body and bride, are heirs to this legacy of OtherWise proclamations. If we consider ourselves part of the Christian church, then we are theologically OtherWise, regardless of our individual gender identity or experience. May we join with the cloud of witnesses who came before us to share this good news!

♡

You are loved. When you are bringing your best self. When they want to change you. When you are able to show them which way to go. When they want to send you away. You are loved.

Chapter 25
Journey with Jesus

Therefore, holy [siblings],
partners in a heavenly calling,
keep your focus
on Jesus,
the apostle and
high priest
of our confession.

Hebrews 3:1
International Standard Version

In 2015, Shannon T.L. Kearns self-published an e-book, called *Walking Toward Resurrection: A Transgender Passion Narrative.* This publication shared from a transgender man's personal journey with Jesus. Kearns models how we might each bring our whole, authentic, transgender self to the sacred stories of the Christian Bible:

> As I began thinking and writing about transgender theology I was simply trying to do something, anything to resurrect my faith. So I began reflecting upon my own experience in light of Scripture. ... I wasn't seeing Jesus as a transgender man or trying to update the story (putting Jesus in a modern context); instead I was seeing how the things that Jesus experienced were echoed in my own experience. ... Writing my own story alongside the Passion narrative has allowed me to wrestle with the text in a new way. It's allowed me to look for points of contact. I've given myself permission to write my story over and into the text. I've seen the text illuminate my life and my life illuminate the text. This interplay of stories has brought me closer to God and brought me back to my faith. I no longer see the Bible as an enemy but as a story that I can find myself in. (Kearns, pages 9–11)

Kearns takes an unapologetic approach to reading scripture as a person of transgender experience and invites us all to go and do likewise:

> For those who are transgender or queer and Christian, I hope this Narrative gives you permission to do your own readings of the Bible, to find yourself in the story of your sacred text. I hope this gives you permission to engage and wrestle and argue. I hope, too, that this gives

> you a connection to Jesus, the one who was always on the side of the marginalized and the outcast. (Kearns, page 11)

This chapter will follow Jesus through several scenes near the end of his (pre-resurrection) life, rewriting the narrative in light of my own OtherWise experiences.

Zey Jesus

My child, Nevaeh, was in fifth grade when I sat her down with my parents to talk about my desire to use "they" and "them" pronouns exclusively. At the time, Nevaeh was still learning grammar and parts of speech in her language arts class at school. She struggled to find the words to explain how it might be a problem to use "they" for one person. Finally, she blurted out, "Can I just call you Zey?!"

We had been talking about my gender for years, so that part of the conversation was not a new revelation at all. Nevaeh wanted to honor my request; she wanted to honor my identity; and she wanted a way to navigate the push-back she might get at school. Her spontaneous response, her creativity in adapting to the situation, and her request for consent all moved me nearly to tears. She taught me a great deal about the connections between love, creativity, and resistance in that moment.

For 24 chapters now, I have dutifully referred to God, Jesus, and even eunuchs with masculine pronouns such as "he" and "him." Yet, I have also touched on the mystery of gender and how God seems to play, relentlessly, with our gendered expectations throughout scripture. With Jesus closely identified with the eunuch (literal or figurative), possibly a parthenogenetic intersex person, or maybe even a new image of the original *ādām* (see chapters 14, 24, and 6 respectively), I am going to go ahead and take the plunge now to explore how it feels to journey with an OtherWise-gendered Jesus who might use pronouns such as, "they," "them," "their," or "zey," "zem," "zir."

Let Anyone Accept This Who Can

In chapter 23, I wrote about the Transfiguration (Matthew 17:1–9; Mark 9:2–9; Luke 9:28–36). When Jesus came down from that mountain, zey was already marching toward zir death. In Matthew 19, Jesus' provocative teaching about eunuchs (see chapter 14) happens as a part of that march. Jesus has already predicted zir own death twice by that point.

Among zir final teachings and healings before the crucifixion and resurrection, Jesus seems to say, "Some of us are different. Some of us are

OtherWise. Some of us are not what you expected, but we are still heirs to the kingdom of God. Let anyone accept this who can."

As someone with a non-binary gender identity, I often find that even people who love me just do not "get it." They may try to use "they" (or "zey") for my pronouns or they may try to remember to add "siblings" when they say "brothers and sisters." What is more rare is for people to really build a different place in their brain for someone who is neither male nor female, but still human. I am not just asking for some creative or *avante garde* adjustment to my pronouns. I am asking folk to adjust the way they think about gender altogether to allow for more nuance and complexity, to allow for more options.

I resonate with Jesus' saying, "Let anyone accept this who can." I know that most of us have been fed the "two and only two" gender model for as long as we can remember. It can be a stretch to change the way we think about "men and women," remembering that God made us human first and added gender later (see chapter 7); remembering that we are fully human, made in the image of God (see chapter 6), even if our gender seems confusing, unexpected, or incomprehensible compared to what we have been taught by mainstream culture.

I have to wonder if Jesus might have been just a little bit exasperated about the whole eunuch thing, when zey finally blurted out something like, "Whatever! You're either going to get it or you won't. But I hope some of you will understand me, if you can."

The Jewish Pride March

Two chapters later, Jesus is out marching in front of everyone as the apparent Grand Marshal of an impromptu Jewish Pride parade, offering zir OtherWise self in a big way (Matthew 21:1–9). Jerusalem was occupied by the Roman Empire, so it was no small thing to go prancing into town with people calling you the son of David (one of the most victorious and revered Jewish kings of all time). This parade was a sign of Jewish solidarity and resistance in the face of an occupying force. This grand entrance was another disruption, with Jesus aligning zemself with the Jewish impulse toward independence.

In the modern world, we often talk about gender as if it is totally different from race, religion, and nationality. Yet, Jesus, like other eunuchs before zem, was not just OtherWise-gendered; zey was also part of a religious and ethnic minority that was surviving under a foreign military occupation. Jesus was not just one thing at a time. Jesus was all of these things at once—a stranger to the Roman Empire as a Jew and stranger to zir own people as a eunuch.

After the parade, the whole city was aflutter, asking, "Who is this?!" Clearly, Jesus made a striking first impression, but this question suggests that there was also something mysterious about zem.

Jesus' defiant entrance into Jerusalem in the face of the Roman occupation should have struck a chord of recognition, not uncertainty. I wonder if this question was less "I don't know who they are!" and more "Who does zey think zey is?!" As noted in chapter 14, eunuchs were looked down upon. So I imagine eunuchs were expected to be bashful and unassuming, not strutting around town like royalty. Maybe it was Jesus' marching, confident and unashamed of zir OtherWise identity, that had people asking, "Who is this person?!"

The House of Jesus

In Jerusalem, Jesus and the disciples gathered in an upper room (*anagaion* in Mark and Luke, *hyperōon* in Acts 1:13) that they found through that "certain" man who was carrying a jar of water (see chapter 24). While they were all guests of the homeowner (*oikodespotē*), Jesus serves as the *de facto* host of this gathering, and we do not know who the house actually belonged to. According to tradition, this is the same room where Jesus washed the disciples' feet (John 13:1–17), where Jesus appeared to a gathering of disciples after zir resurrection (Luke 24:36–49), and where the Pentecost gathering occurred (Acts 2). It was a private space, since it was upstairs, but it was also a very large room (called *mega* in Mark and Luke)—large enough to hold a large crowd at Pentecost. Some scholars argue that this upper room was where Jesus and the disciples stayed, or at least gathered, when they were in Jerusalem.

In the previous chapter, I noted that this "certain" man appears to have been an OtherWise-gendered person, possibly a literal eunuch and/or one of the celibate Essenes (a figurative eunuch). So was this a house of eunuchs (literal or figurative)? Was it an Essene community? Had Jesus met with someone from this "certain" household separate from the disciples? Did a prior relationship with this "certain" household have anything to do with Jesus' teaching about eunuchs (see chapter 14)? What happened during (or after) the Last Supper so that the disciples kept coming back for their regular gatherings (and possibly even stayed there)?

Scholars suggest that John the Baptist (who is seen as a pre-cursor to Jesus) was an Essene. We do not know a lot about the Essenes, but they are described by several first century CE writers. Jewish historian Josephus identified the Essenes as one of three major sects (with Pharisees and Sadducees) of Judaism at that time. The Roman writer Pliny suggested that the Essenes were celibate and unmarried men (though Josephus indicated that some Essene communities allowed marriage). Essenes would live in community without any personal property and were extremely devout. Philo wrote that the Essenes completely avoided slavery, animal sacrifices, commerce, and military endeavors. Essene communities are considered precursors to the monastic communities of the early Christian church—connecting them back to "eunuchs for the sake of the kingdom" (see chapter 17) in another way.

OtherWise-gendered folk know a lot about chosen family. When your family of origin does not understand you or does not want you, there is something powerful about creating a new family—a family that is not necessarily sexual or romantic in nature. This is often how we "choose life" (see chapter 1). OtherWise-gendered folk often cling to one another in love and in hope, in contrast to a world that sees us as undesirable or even dangerous.

Ballroom culture emerges from a small community in the U.S. (especially in the Northeast) that frequently serves as a safer space for Black and Latinx same-gender-loving, transgender, and gender non-conforming young people. Individuals compete at events known as "balls." A ball contestant typically walks, dances, or vogues in various categories and is judged based on their appearance, including costume, dance moves, and overall attitude. Ballroom communities have come to be somewhat better known in mainstream culture through the documentary film *Paris Is Burning* (1990) and the scripted TV drama *Pose* (2018–2019).

In ballroom communities, individuals may join (or be adopted into) a "House" which is organized around a parent figure and their (adult) children. The "House" gathers its "children" in and keeps them from living alone on the streets. The parent of the "House" provides loving care, discipline, and purpose for the children as well as survival resources. While a "House" is not typically a legal family relationship, it is not accurate to call it an "informal" structure, either. A "House" is an intimate and substantial family structure that is based on neither marriage nor biology and that supports the well-being and survival of its members.

I am imagining that this "certain" household in Jerusalem may have been a pre-existing Essene community in Jerusalem, but that it was transformed into the "House of Jesus" (Live, Work, POSE!!) with the disciples as elder siblings. Jesus introduced the disciples to this "certain" household, just hours before zey would be arrested and condemned to die on the cross. The "upper room" apparently became a base for the disciples and the early Christian community in those first weeks after Jesus' death and resurrection. Reimagining this otherwise unnamed "upper room" as the gathering place for Jesus' chosen family structure, for the "House of Jesus" (Dip, Pop, Spin!!), brings out the intimacy and vulnerability of the way these Jesus-followers came together. In those first weeks, they were not building a religious institution at all. They were simply clinging to one another, in love and in hope, in contrast to a world that had just killed their beloved Jesus. They were surviving and they were taking refuge in one another.

Gathering Broken Pieces

Jesus brought the disciples to the "upper room" for a final meal together (Matthew 26:26–29; Mark 14:22–25; Luke 22:14–20; 1 Corinthians 11:23–26) at this pivotal moment which has come to be called "The Last Supper." While they gathered in the season of Passover, it would be anachronistic to understand the last supper as a Jewish seder because the seder traditions emerged later. The remembrance of this meal would go on to become a central metaphor of Christianity, called alternately "Holy Communion," the "Lord's Supper," or the "Eucharist." It is an iconic event that has been interpreted and re-interpreted, on a daily basis for 2,000 years as an essential ritual of the church.

Jesus had already had many iconic meals. Zey turned water into wine (John 2:1–11); zey fed the multitudes with loaves and fishes (Matthew 14:13–21; John 6:1–14); and zey caused a stir by eating with "tax collectors and sinners" (Matthew 9:10–12; Mark 2:15–17; Luke 5:29–32). This last supper draws all of those images together in a climactic moment, as Jesus breaks the bread, pours the wine, and shares a meal with zir disciples.

This meal together is how we remember that the "House of Jesus" (Sashay your way, beloved!!) is a house for eunuchs, foreigners, and strangers—for OtherWise, freaks, and weirdos—to come together and be fed. We remember that Jesus is a eunuch (see chapter 14), the firstborn among many siblings (Romans 8:29)—yet, not the kind of eunuch who is a slave living in fear (Romans 8:15) under a foreign occupation! We remember that there is no shame in being broken and poured out like Jesus, as we cling to one another in love and in hope. We, too, are adopted children, heirs to the kingdom, kindred family with all who cry out to the Parent of the "House of Jesus."

J Mase III writes as a survivor of both intimate and religious violence in his book, *And Then I Got Fired: One Transqueer's Reflections on Grief, Unemployment & Inappropriate Jokes About Death* (2019):

> Pastor,
> Tell whoever you been praying to
> this is my body
> It has been broken from what your
> followers
> have done to me
> This blood has been spilled

in Remembrance of you

J Mase III, *And Then I Got Fired*, page 61
(Check the bibliography for spoken word version!)

At the Last Supper, Jesus invites us to boldly bring our bloody pain and broken bodies to be shared with our OtherWise family as we remember Zey Jesus and recommit to being slaves no more.

Hard Choices: Betrayal, Denial, and Despair

I wrote about the relationship between Judas and Jesus in chapter 23 as an example of Jesus' humanity, but when I read about Judas' suicide (Matthew 27:1–10), I cannot help but think about transgender communities. The statistics about suicidal ideation and attempted suicide among people of transgender experience are mind-boggling. Yet, I can testify to the despair that comes from feeling like you do not belong anywhere—that comes from feeling like you have nowhere left to turn.

We really do not know why Judas betrayed Jesus, but we do know that all 12 of the disciples would eventually abandon zem (Mark 14:50). Even Peter, "the rock," denied knowing Jesus three times (Matthew 26:69–75; Mark 14:66–72; Luke 22:54–62) once this final act was in motion. Judas was not alone in struggling with what Peter Enns calls the "surprise ending" of the Jesus story (Enns, pages 195 and 199).

What do you do when the whole city is murmuring against you? What do you do when the "powers that be" approach you with a proposal that they say will spare lives, sacrificing the one for the many? What do you do when it seems like you have no safe harbor—nowhere left to turn? Like the eunuchs who betrayed Jezebel (see chapter 16) and the eunuchs who planned to assassinate King Xerxes (also chapter 16), Judas was caught up in the politics of the day and forced to take a side.

Arranging for the arrest of Jesus probably did save Jerusalem. Folk were stirred up after Jesus' grand entrance. Those who were conspiring against Jesus were specifically trying to avoid causing a riot (Matthew 26:3–5; Mark 14:1–2), which suggests this was a city on the brink. At least one Jesus follower had a sword and was more than ready to fight ("With that, one of Jesus' companions reached for his sword, drew it out and struck the servant of the high priest, cutting off his ear." Matthew 26:51 NIV; Mark 14:47; in John 18:10 it was Peter). Jesus had tried to prepare them, but nobody really seemed to catch zir vision until it was all over. Jerusalem was on edge and ready to boil over in riots or a full-blown insurrection.

I am not trying to spare Judas from our judgment. History has made him a villain. However, I am trying to imagine what it would have been like for him as Jesus entered Jerusalem. Transgender communities are often faced with few productive options. We do what we can to survive. Sometimes we live at the margins, working in survival economies that may have us breaking the law and putting our lives at risk just to get by. Sometimes we align ourselves with people who are ready to use and abuse us for their own purposes, because that seems like our best option. When you have nowhere else to turn, these are really hard choices. Judas seems to have been faced with just such a moment.

In Luke 22:3a (also John 13:27), we are told that "Satan entered into Judas Iscariot." I am reminded that when Peter was ready to fight for Jesus, Jesus rebuked him with, "Get behind me, Satan!" (Matthew 16:23a). With 2,000 years of hindsight, it is easy to lose track of how confusing it must have been for the disciples, trying to figure out what Jesus was aiming for. Was zey trying to start a riot? Was Jesus claiming zir place as rightful heir to King David? Was Jesus leading them all to the slaughter, defiant vagabonds versus the army of the Roman Empire?

The stories point us toward the turmoil among Jesus, Peter, and Judas, but, in this march toward crucifixion, the real problem is colonization. The real problem is the power dynamics that make it unbearable to live in the shadow of an all-powerful empire that does not have your best interests in mind. Jesus, the disciples, and all of the Jewish people at that time were dominated by an outside power that enforced its will by military force. The occupation pressed even the religious leaders of the day to make hard choices about their loyalty and their options for survival.

We can judge their choices as we will, but let us not lose sight of the way colonization created and shaped their options in the first place. Judas probably thought he was navigating a "lose-lose" situation. I believe that he was struggling with worry and despair about the way government authorities would retaliate against all of Jerusalem, if Jesus continued on this collision course, taunting both the religious and the political authorities. Judas made his choice.

Alone

As Judas's betrayal was unfolding, Jesus went with the other disciples to the garden at Gethsemane (Matthew 26:36–46; Mark 14:32–42; Luke 22:40–46). This time, it was Jesus, not Nicodemus, laying awake at night struggling with anxiety (see chapter 23). Jesus wants the comfort and company of zir friends, but they fall asleep on Jesus over and over again. There are some things that we just have to do by ourselves.

No matter how much someone loves me, there are certain truths that are mine and mine alone to bear. Each one of us is part of the body of Christ (1 Corinthians 12:12–14; Ephesians 4:1–16). Each one of us is a partial reflection of the image of God (Genesis 1:27). No one can replace what is special and unique about you. No one can give your testimony except you. Others may support, encourage, and accompany us on the journey, but sometimes standing out from the crowd is a heavy burden that we must bear on our own. Sometimes the very gift of being extraordinary can feel like a cross you have to bear. Like a good House Mother, Jesus says, "Pick that thing up and walk. Werq it!"

Cut Off

Jesus died on a cross. Jesus was killed by the Roman Empire. Jesus was a convicted criminal who was executed. In the Roman Empire, the cross was the death penalty. There was no constitution preventing "cruel and unusual punishment." Provocateurs would be made into very public examples. They would be hung up to die a slow and gruesome death as a spectacle and as a warning. As the literal eunuch had body part(s) cut off, as anyone without children was cut off from family and community and thus the future, as slaves and foreigners would be cut off from their own people to become resident aliens in someone else's kingdom, Jesus was killed as a condemned criminal, convicted blasphemer, and political renegade (see chapter 13). Zey was cut off.

It is tricky about all this death and suffering. There is a critical difference between acknowledging that the world causes suffering and celebrating that suffering as inherently good. There is a difference between taking away the shame of such a humiliation and making humiliation a badge of honor. Kearns puts it this way,

> Let me say in no uncertain terms; suffering is not to be glorified, especially when someone is being made to suffer at the hands of someone else. That isn't cause for celebration, it is cause for outrage. It is oppression and abuse, plain and simple. To tell someone that they must endure their situation as "bearing a cross" is bad theology. (Kearns, page 24)

Many people twist Jesus' encouragement to "take up your cross" (Matthew 10:38, 16:24; Mark 8:34; Luke 9:23, 14:27) to mean you should willingly submit yourself to exploitation and abuse. "Enjoy your suffering!" they seem to suggest, but that is not it at all. Jesus also lifts up this saying, "I desire mercy, not sacrifice" (Matthew 9:13a and 12:7, citing Hosea 6:6). Jesus does not desire suffering. Zey only acknowledges that we will need to face hard choices as we become true to our most authentic selves in a merciless world.

We can never appreciate resurrection without first taking the crucifixion seriously. Jesus' crucifixion is a victory for deceit, for empire, for despair, for death. It is painful and humiliating. It is not a pretty path to redemption. It is torture. This death is the ultimate defeat and a warning for those who would imitate Jesus. It is only when we fully accept this horror that the testimony of resurrection power can begin to make sense. "Take up your cross" is an invitation to face off defiantly with all of the powers of death and despair, knowing you are never actually alone—knowing there are some things that Death cannot steal away.

In Between, After, and Before

Jesus is dead (Matthew 27:50; Mark 15:37; Luke 23:46; John 19:30). Judas has betrayed Jesus. Peter has denied Jesus. The disciples have scattered. It is tempting to rush on to resurrection, but these moments may be the ones that are most important for us to sit with. Only a few stayed: Mother Mary, Aunt Mary, Mary the wife of Clopas, and Mary Magdalene at the foot of the cross with the beloved disciple (John 19:25–27, also Luke 23:27, 23:49); Nicodemus and Joseph of Arimathea tending zir body (John 19:38–39, also Matthew 27:57–60; Mark 14: 43–46; Luke 23:50–53); Mary Magdalene and other women going to the tomb expecting to find a corpse (Matthew 28:1; Mark 16:1; Luke 24:1; John 20:1). What do we do with our grief and our fear and our rage in moments of humiliation and defeat, like these? Do we run away? Do we hide? Do we stay and weep with loved ones? Do we honor the fallen?

Despair is powerful. Even when a hope-filled testimony comes, most of the disciples refuse to believe the good news (Luke 24:10–11). When Jesus appears in their midst, they are still frightened (Luke 24:36–37; John 20:19). We, too, live in this in-between world after the crucifixion, where despair rules. We cannot quite take it in when good news does arrive. We are frightened and afraid. These are reasonable responses to the way the world operates, both then and now. Empire has the upper hand. Death is real, and despair reigns.

Some theologians like to talk about the "already and not yet" of resurrection. Jesus has come. We are still here. The world goes on with its misery. We are in-between, after, and before—all out of order and making no sense.

Still Fucking Here

Jesus shows up inexplicably: in locked rooms filled with fear (John 20:19; Luke 24:36), in our grief and mourning (John 20:11–14), in table fellowship with our siblings (Luke 24:30; John 21:1–14), bearing witness to broken and bloody bodies, in the community meals where we remember and re-member, in the moments where we are putting ourselves and our families back together after an assault. Jesus shows up in *those* places saying "Peace be with you" (John 20:19; or "Rejoice!" in Matthew 28:9).

The incomparable Miss Major Griffin-Gracy, has survived as a Black transgender woman for 50 years after participating in the Stonewall riots of 1969. Mother Major's signature closing comment is "I'm still fucking here." Like those who have whitewashed and commercialized the Stonewall riots, religious leaders and politicians have long been working to domesticate Zey Jesus into a tidy religious icon. However, zey was a radical who confronted respectability, bringing us this promise: Death will not have the ultimate victory. Jesus reaches out to us, with a tender defiance like unto our beloved Mother Major, saying, "I love you, baby, and I'm still fucking here. We got this."

We have been given so many sacred stories of Love and Resistance. We speak of the Divine working in our lives. If we are not manly men, our lived experience is dismissed as "unbelievable" or "not credible" (Mark 16:11; Luke 24:11). Born of this struggle, we are already dangerous if we simply dare to exist out in the open. We are magical earth creatures, who have been written out of existence. They have been organizing to make us disappear for centuries. They want us to live in despair and humiliation, as slaves to Death. Of course, we are tempted to hide and to conform. We go along to get along.

Yet, Zey Jesus shows us another way. Zey Jesus made people uncomfortable. Zey stirred things up. Zey lived defiantly. Zey loved extravagantly. Zey showed up even after all was lost in the most humiliating of defeats imaginable. Zey shows up in those dark, lonely, fear-filled places inviting us to boldly carry on. Let anyone accept this who can. I hope you will understand me.

Full disclosure: I do not identify as "Christian" anymore. That word has been so misused and abused—so cloaked in violence that it just does not make any sense to me anymore. Yet, the good news of the resurrection still speaks to me. This story has claimed me and changed me. This story is my story and the story of my people. This is the story of my elders and our ancestors. This is the story of my children and the Young Leaders who are yet to come.

I am a witness to the resurrection. I am OtherWise and I have come to testify about this new creation where there is no male and female, slave nor free, Jew nor Gentile—where there is neither Queer nor straight, Black nor white, Native-born nor colonizer, legal nor illegal, binary nor non-binary, cisgender nor transgender, able or disabled.

I cannot explain it. It makes no sense. It is nonsense—like an old barren woman who gives birth to a new baby (see chapter 18). It is laughable and ridiculous. Yet, this is the hope to which we testify. I have no interest in arguing over what "really" happened after Jesus died. All I know is that I have seen zem walking among us and I can do no other. I am here to tell the story and bear witness to the truth of it. I believe. God help my unbelief.

Zey lives. Zey walks with me. Zey talks with me. Zey tells me that I belong with zem. Zey is not dead. Zey is alive. Zey is still fucking here after two millennia of religious and political shenanigans that tried to take zem away from us. This is a miracle. This is our resurrection promise. Zey is risen. Zey is risen, indeed.

♡

You are loved. When you want to riot. When you cling to your chosen family. When you are alone or cut off. When none of it makes any sense. When they do not believe you. You are loved.

You are loved. When you remember. When you testify. When you tell the story. When you bear witness. When you gather up the broken pieces. When you are still fucking here. You are loved.

Epilogue
Living OtherWise Ever After

"For I know the plans
I have for you,"
declares the LORD,
"plans to prosper you
and not to harm you,
plans to give you
hope and a future."

Jeremiah 29:11 NIV

I believe that the Christian Bible is full of OtherWise-gendered characters doing God's work in the world. I believe that Jesus Christ was OtherWise and encouraged us to boldly testify to OtherWise ways of being. I believe that the world will respond to our testimonies with fear and even violence, just as they responded to Jesus. Yet, Zey Jesus shows us how to resist those who prefer a domesticated, "meek and mild," whitewashed Jesus who tells us to conform—who would have us hide our OtherWise gifts just so others might be comfortable.

I do not believe that we have to be a "perfect" anything in order to experience God's grace. We get to be human, messy, mixed up and out of order. That is ok! God will take care of the rest. I believe in the promise of resurrection. I believe that there are many ways to be OtherWise and that without all of our diverse testimonies, the image of God and body of Christ are diminished. I believe that when we gather our broken pieces together and remember the divine, something magical happens—something we call the power of the resurrection.

Listening to Our Bodies

One of the key features of the longstanding men vs. unmen hierarchy is the pathologizing of the body. The idea that the body is the root of our problems takes many forms, from the policing of desire to the devaluing of our emotional lives more generally to treating unmen as dangerous or defective. Entire categories of human experience are written off as being "base pursuits" that are negatively associated with the body. In this approach, our "thinking thoughts" are almost the only thing that matters.

Part and parcel to this argument is the idea that women, children, and other unmen need to be controlled and dominated (along with all of the non-human creation) because they are allegedly less able to control their base instincts, their feelings, their bodies. The "kind of, sort of" empowering teaching that women can "become men" (see chapter 24) is still connected to the idea that only manly men can rise above the trappings of this fallen world. It is only a partial win for unmen because manly men are still considered the ideal, even if a woman's body is not seen as inherently and entirely disqualifying.

Being OtherWise is not just about resisting the gender I was assigned at birth. It also means that I am learning to value my body, the wisdom that it holds, and the stories that it tells. When the risen Jesus appeared to Thomas, zey showed him the scars on zir body (John 20:24–29). Jesus was not resurrected into a new, perfect, spiritual body. Jesus was resurrected into zir same broken body that was somehow miraculously given new life. The new creation in Christ is not about leaving our bodies (or the so-called "trappings" of unmen) behind. It is about bringing new life to all that we already have.

So many of us have been taught to hate our bodies, for one reason or another. This is not only a function of the men vs. unmen hierarchy but also a function of the modern advertising industry, which invests heavily in defining "problems" in order that they might sell us their "solutions" (also known as products). Yet, our bodies are more than just leverage for propping up our self-esteem. Our bodies tell our stories. They hold not only scars but also our pain and our deepest longings. Our bodies are a physical link to our ancestors and a tangible means for giving and receiving love. Our bodies are a sacred text, a record of where we have been as well as what has been done to us. Our bodies are the primary way we experience God's good creation.

In a modern world of medical interventions, those of us with financial means have more choices than ever about how to live into these bodies—from medicines to hormones, from surgical to even genetic interventions. Transgender people are often derided for changing our bodies, though other medical procedures are not held up to the same harsh criticism. The critical ethical question always seems to be about who gets to decide. Are we forcing medical procedures on people who may not want them (for example, sterilization or "corrective" intersex surgeries)? Or, are individuals being supported in bringing new life to their bodies? Are we pressing extraordinary human earth creatures to conform to cookie-cutter ideas about how a body is supposed to look? Or, are we compassionately embracing each and every body as an unfolding story of grace?

Jesus came not as a disembodied spirit but as a fully human, physical body. Theologians call this the "incarnation," which means that

"God took on human flesh," in order that zey might be fully with us, experiencing a full range of feelings and embodied experiences. In other words, God chose to use a human body to connect with us, to relate to us, and to deliver a message of love! Learning to love our bodies is a radical act of resistance. It does not mean that we can never make changes to our bodies. It just means that we need to care for and listen to all the wisdom our bodies have to offer us.

Listening to Sacred Text

I have now written an entire book about the Christian Bible, which begs the question of why this ancient book matters so much. There are many sacred texts that were not included in the canon. In other words, as the years went on, certain people in certain communities decided which stories, letters, and documents would be put together as "the Bible." Many stories and documents (such as the *Gospel of Thomas*, mentioned in chapter 24) were also left out. The books that did make it in are a messy collection of odds and ends, filled with different forms and sometimes even messages that seem contradictory.

In my white, professional class up-bringing (specifically in the Reformed branch of Protestant Christianity), I learned to take Christian text and tradition seriously. There were rules to be followed and mysteries to be solved, but the emphasis was on knowledge and belief. It was up to me to get it "right." It mattered that these books of the Bible were the "right" ones. In that framework, it was troubling to learn that there were also "other" sacred books.

In my later years, I have been increasingly connected to Black Church communities. In those communities, I have come to understand the Bible as an ancestral tradition. It is not just that someone a long time ago decided that these books were important or the "right" ones. It is also important, and perhaps even more so, that all kinds of people have been engaging these texts for many generations, finding strength and sustenance along the way. When we engage with sacred text, we are engaging with the ancestors and with communities of resistance through the ages. The text itself is a way that we have a shared experience with Christians who lived hundreds of years ago, with our parents and grandparents in faith, and with our children who are yet to come.

Obviously, Christian text and tradition have also been used by slave-owners and anti-gay bigots and others who seek to justify making others "less than." There is a long history of appropriation of Christian text and tradition by those who wish to dominate, control, and subdue. See appendix C for a beginning discussion of "Christendom" and the way

Christianity came to be used as a tool of empire. But, the (often popular) interpretations used to support violence are just one version of the story. The word "heresy" originally referred only to a difference of opinion. However, as disagreements grew antagonistic and particular views were enforced by both religious and government authorities, "heresy" became a bludgeon and "heretic" became a slur. We need to reclaim the strength that comes from offering a different point of view.

Because of that history, it has been essential for me to read scripture in community with others who are concerned with liberation. My understanding of biblical justice expanded as I was exposed to Catholic Workers, Mennonites, Quakers, and other justice-minded Christians who were taking the Bible seriously in ways that were new to me. I have learned a great deal about Christian tradition from Jewish and Muslim siblings. My understanding of Christian resistance has changed as a result of my experiencing embodied worship in predominantly Black Church settings, where feeling and expressing our feelings is part of finding a way through the world we live in. Modern-day OtherWise-gendered people are by no means the first to have taken back the Bible from those who would use it to harm others.

My white, professional-class, Christian up-bringing did not teach me to survive in a world that does not want me to exist. I have learned and am learning that from Black, Indigenous, and other People of Color, from Jews and Muslims, from transgender and gender non-conforming people, from disabled and differently-abled people, and from others who struggle. If you are only reading scripture in community with people of privilege and means, then Jesus may be calling you, like Nicodemus (see chapter 23), to get out of your comfort zone to be born again. Are you receiving the witness of all of those who are struggling to survive in this world (John 3:11)? Appendix B lists a variety of books that may help you to find some alternative perspectives. However, nothing can replace the experience of being in community with those who have a different story than yours. There are some things that are truly written into our bodies, and it is rare that a book can begin to capture those aspects. Being face-to-face with those who have struggled to survive is the only way to truly move beyond stereotypes and caricatures to experience the power of Christian tradition(s) alive in community.

Many Voices, One Body

There is not one monolithic Christian tradition but, rather, many Christian traditions. While modern public discourse too often proceeds as if there were one and only one Christian consensus position on all matters of controversy, Christianity is actually full of epic internal disagreements. Our history is filled with religiously motivated violence, particularly (but not only) between Catholics, Protestants, and Anabaptists in the Western world. Black Church expressions of Christianity have diverged from white Christian orthodoxy in significant and important ways. There are multiple different ways to read the Bible and understand Christian tradition.

This is another place where Christians have much to learn from our Jewish kin. In contrast to the way that Christianity became increasingly hierarchical and dogmatic after Emperor Constantine's conversion and the Council of Nicea (see appendix C), Rabbinic Judaism is self-consciously multivocal. In her online article, "Can We Talk? Building a Spirit of 'Sacred Disagreement' on Israel," Melissa Weintraub argues that, while Jews certainly have their own patterns of avoidance and antagonism, a "dominant strand of Jewish tradition" is *mahloket l'shem shamayim* or "sacred disagreement." Weintraub cites several ancient texts in support of this thesis:

> One voice divided into seven voices and these into 70 languages. (Exodus Rabba 28:6)
>
> Just as a hammer [stroke] scatters many sparks, so a single Scriptural passage yields many senses. (BT Sanhedrin 34a)
>
> The scroll of the Torah is [written] without vowels, in order to enable man to interpret it however he wishes... as the consonants without the vowels bear several interpretations, and [may be] divided into several sparks. (Bahya ben Asher, *Commentary on the Torah*, Num. 11:15)

In other words, there is nothing wrong with having multiple interpretations of a text or even the Mosaic law. Weitraub continues, indicating that this pluralistic mindset

> does demand of us intellectual humility—embrace of our limitations and uncertainty, recognition that truth cannot be known through only one voice but rather only through rigorous search and deliberation. (Weintraub)

I have had to unlearn this thing about needing to be "right," so that I can better listen for the insights that come from new and different interpretations of sacred text and tradition. A multivocal tradition is one that is collaborative and generative—one that recognizes "disagreements as signposts" for important questions and "springboards to greater intelligence" (Weintraub). We need not pretend that all perspectives are "equally convincing or valid" (Weintraub) but only that there is strength to be gained in the considering of diverse viewpoints. We should be engaging sacred text, not because we desire power or dominance, but in a common search for knowledge and wisdom.

This is just the kind of pluralistic unity that happened at Pentecost (Acts 2). Jesus had already ascended into heaven; the disciples were gathered again in the "upper room;" and there was "a violent rushing wind," "tongues of fire," and the arrival of the Holy Spirit. A crowd gathered as they heard the sound of these many different voices, but each with understanding (Acts 2:6). The scripture does not say that they were all saying the same thing. Rather, there were many testimonies, and everyone was able to be understood, regardless of the language that was being used.

An OtherWise Christianity welcomes this Pentecost ethic, believing that we are better for having heard from each of these different voices. If we bring the requisite humility, we need not be divided by "sacred disagreements." Despite a history of violent schism, the Christian tradition is already *de facto* multivocal, as is the Christian Bible. Even Paul writes, "There are... so many kinds of voices in the world, and none of them is without meaning" (1 Corinthians 14:10 King James 2000 Bible). The truth does not come in a singular voice. Layers of wisdom become more clear through a diversity of expression and layers of interpretation.

A Cloud of Witnesses

In the 25 chapters of *OtherWise Christian: A Guidebook for Transgender Liberation*, I have drawn on a wide array of authors and scholars who have commented on the Christian Bible and its relationship to gender. I am grateful for this cloud of witnesses (Hebrews 12:1), who have taken the time to wrestle with the text(s) and share their insights with the world. I am similarly inspired by friends and colleagues who have shared the sacred text of their lives with me in ways that have influenced my writing.

You, as a reader, are also part of this cloud of witnesses. You, too, will read and wrestle and, hopefully, respond. As I said in the preface, it is not my goal to make you a "proper" Christian. You do not have to agree with me! I do hope that I have offered some insights that will help you navigate Christian trans-antagonism. Perhaps you will even go back to the text of the Bible and/or of your own life to reflect further. However my writing has landed with you, I hope that you will boldly share your insights with the communities of which you are a part.

I have several ideas for publishing follow-up books, several of which will be anthologies highlighting writing from OtherWise authors on themes related to this book. I know that I have only scratched the surface of OtherWise insights in this initial project. I am particularly interested in sharing more reflections and insights from intersex people, non-binary people, multi-lingual people, disabled and differently-abled people, Catholics, Mormons, Jews, and Muslims, as well as people who are Black, Indigenous, or otherwise People of Color. My ultimate hope and desire is to support the next generation of leaders in taking this work to the next level.

How is your experience reflected in the Christian Bible? Where do you find resonance among the stories of our ancestors in faith? What OtherWise Bible stories have I missed? How would you approach these topics differently? What are your strategies for resisting the "two and only two" gender paradigm? What are your strategies for bringing healing to the broken places you have witnessed?

You certainly do not have to be a pastor or a priest, a professor or a scholar to be a part of the resistance! Indeed, we need more dreamers and dancers, poets and lovers, sacred prophets and OtherWise disruptors. I would love to hear from you. Please be in touch at otherwise.christian@gmail.com. You can check http://www.otherwisechristian.com for the latest news about my call for submissions and follow-up publications and projects.

♡

You are loved. When you are living in your body. When you are wrestling in community. When you are sharing the sacred text of your life. You are loved.

May we remember that we have already come a long way. Come what may, let us not forget one another or the grace that has brought us together. You are loved.

Amen. Blessed be. Thanks be to God!

Bibliography

An informal bibliography of works cited or recommended. Organized by category and date of publication. Unless another edition is noted, my in-chapter references are from the original work, not later editions.

General Transgender Historical

Another Mother Tongue: Gay Words, Gay Worlds (1984 and 1990) by Judy Grahn

Transgender Warriors : Making History from Joan of Arc to Dennis Rodman (1996) by Leslie Feinberg

Transgender History: The Roots of Today's Revolution (2008 and 2017) by Susan Stryker

Black on Both Sides: A Racial History of Trans Identity (2017) by C. Riley Snorton

General Transgender Liberation

Trans Liberation: Beyond Pink or Blue (1992) by Leslie Feinberg

Gender Outlaw: On Men, Women, and the Rest of Us (1994 and 2016) by Kate Bornstein

My Gender Workbook: How to Become a Real Man, a Real Woman, the Real You, or Something Else Entirely (1998) by Kate Bornstein

Gender Outlaws: The Next Generation (2010) by Kate Bornstein and S. Bear Bergman

My New Gender Workbook: A Step-by-Step Guide to Achieving World Peace through Gender Anarchy and Sex Positivity (2013) by Kate Bornstein

Major! (2015) documentary film about Miss Major Griffin-Gracy

Hebrew Scripture and Jewish Tradition

The JPS Torah Commentary: Genesis (1989) by Nahum M Sarna

Judges (2000) by Tammi J. Schneider

Reading the Women of the Bible: A New Interpretation of Their Stories (2002) by Tikva Frymer-Kensky

Jacob's Wound: Homoerotic Narrative in the Literature of Ancient Israel (2005) by Theodore W. Jennings, Jr.

"Terms for Gender Diversity in Classical Jewish Texts" (2006) by Elliot Kukla from *TransTorah* resource list (published by TransTorah, http://www.transtorah.org)

TransTexts (website, launched 2008) by Reuben Zellman and Elliot Kukla (now available in the Keshet resource section, https://www.keshetonline.org/resources/)

Daughters of Miriam: Women Prophets in Ancient Israel (2008) by Wilda C. Gafney

"When Gender Varies: A Curious Case of Kere and Ketiv, Parashat Chayei Sarah (Genesis 23:1–25:18)" by Rachel Brodie in *Torah Queeries: Weekly Commentaries on the Hebrew Bible* (2009), edited by Lesser Joshua, Gregg Drinkwater, and Joshua Lesser

"Joseph's Fabulous Technicolor Dreamcoat: Parashat Vayeshev (Genesis 37:1–40:23)" by Gregg Drinkwater in *Torah Queeries: Weekly Commentaries on the Hebrew Bible* (2009), edited by Lesser Joshua, Gregg Drinkwater, and Joshua Lesser

"Male and Female God Created Them: Parashat Bereshit (Genesis 1:1–6:8)" by Margaret Moers Wenig in *Torah Queeries: Weekly Commentaries on the Hebrew Bible* (2009), edited by Lesser Joshua, Gregg Drinkwater, and Joshua Lesser

Balancing on the Mechitza: Transgender in the Jewish Community (2010), edited by Noach Dzmura

"The God Thing" by Joy Ladin in *Balancing on the Mechitza: Transgender in the Jewish Community* (2010), edited by Noach Dzmura

"Judaism and Gender Issues" by Beth Orens in *Balancing on the Mechitza: Transgender in the Jewish Community* (2010), edited by Noach Dzmura

"I'm Just Not That Kind of God: Queering Kabbalistic Gender Play" by Jay Michaelson in *Queer Religion* (2011), edited by Donald Boisvert and Jay Johnson

"Can We Talk? Building a Spirit of 'Sacred Disagreement' on Israel" (2013) by Melissa Weintraub (published by the Shalom Hartman Institute, http://www.hartman.org.il)

"The 'Aylonit' in Jewish Legal Context," (2015) by Melvin Marsh (published by Sojourn, http://www.sojourngsd.org)

"Transgender Jews and Halakhah," by Leonard A. Sharzer (adopted by the Committee on Jewish Law and Standards of the [Conservative] Rabbinical Assembly on June 7, 2017), available at http://www.rabbinicalassembly.org as transgender-halakhah.pdf

Womanist Midrash: A Reintroduction to the Women of the Torah and the Throne (2017) by Wilda C. Gafney

"A Torah Lesson on Gender with Abby Stein" (2018) by Abby Stein on YouTube (https://www.youtube.com/watch?v=cfd9R70jtc4)

The Soul of the Stranger: Reading God and Torah from a Transgender Perspective (2019) by Joy Ladin

Eunuch-Specific

"The Celibacy Legion in Matthew 19:12" by Jerome Kodell in *Biblical Theology Bulletin: Journal of Bible and Culture* (1978)

Eunuchen als Sklaven und freigelassene in der griechisch-romischen Antike (1980), by Peter Guyot

Slavery and Social Death: A Comparative Study (1982) by Orlando Patterson

Gender, Power, and Promise: The Subject of the Bible's First Story (1992) by David M. Gunn and Danna Nolan Fewell

"The Concubine and the Eunuch: Queering Up the Breeder's Bible" by Victoria Kolakowski in *Our Families, Our Values: Snapshots of Queer Kinship* (1997), edited by Robert E. Goss and Amy Adams Squire Strongheart

"'Do You Understand What You Are Reading?' A Reading of the Ethiopian Eunuch Story (Acts 8.26–40) from a Site of Cultural Marronage" (1999 dissertation, Union Theological Seminary, New York, NY) by Cottrel R. Carson

"Throwing a Party: Patriarchy, Gender, and the Death of Jezebel" by Victoria Kolakowski in *Take Back the Word: A Queer Reading of the Bible* (2000), edited by Robert E. Goss and Mona West

Castration: An Abbreviated History of Western Manhood (2000) by Gary Taylor

Eunuchs and Castrati: A Cultural History by Piotr O. Scholz (translated 2001 by Broadwin and Frisch)

The Manly Eunuch: Masculinity, Gender Ambiguity, and Christian Ideology in Late Antiquity (2001) by Mathew Kuefler

"The Hidden Eunuchs of the Hebrew Bible: Uncovering an Alternate Gender" (2003 dissertation, Iliff School of Theology and University of Denver, Colorado Seminary) by Janet Everhart

"What Is to Prevent Me from Being Baptized? Reading beyond the Readily Apparent" by Tolonda Henderson in the *Chicago Theological Seminary Register* (2003)

The Perfect Servant: Eunuchs and the Social Construction of Gender in Byzantium (2003) by Kathryn Ringrose

"Towards a Transgender Theology: Que(e)rying the Eunuchs" by Lewis Reay in *Trans/formations* (2009), edited by Marcella Althaus-Reid and Lisa Isherwood

"Complex Identities: Ethnicities, Gender, and Religion in the Story of the Ethiopian Eunuch (Acts 8:26–40)" by Marianne Bjelland Kartzow and Halvor Moxnes in *Religion and Theology* (2010)

"Eunuch-Inclusive Esther—Queer Theology 101" (2013) by Peterson Toscano (published at https://petersontoscano.wordpress.com)

Queering the Ethiopian Eunuch: Strategies of Ambiguity in Acts (2013) by Sean D. Burke

"Falling for Ebed Melech" by Peterson Toscano in *Rainbow in the Word: LGBTQ Christians' Biblical Memoirs* (2017), edited by Ellin Sterne Jimmerson. See also "Revealed! A Gender Variant Savior" on Peterson Toscano's YouTube channel.

Christian Scripture and Tradition

Church Dogmatics (1932) by Karl Barth

The Church and the Homosexual (1976 first edition, 1993 fourth edition) by John J. McNeill

"A Proposed Biological Interpretation of the Virgin Birth" by Edward Kessel in *Journal of American Scientific Affiliation* (1983)

"Luke's Geographical Horizon" by James M. Scott in *The Book of Acts in Its First Century Setting (Book 2)* (1994), edited by David W. J. Gill and Conrad Gempf

Our Tribe: Queer Folks, God, Jesus, and the Bible (1995 and 2000) by Nancy Wilson

Making the Difference: Gender, Personhood, and Theology (1996) by Elaine Graham

Acts (1997), by F. Scott Spencer

"Transsexual Theology" (1997) by Starchild (published by *Whosoever* magazine, http://www.whosoever.org)

"Toward a Christian Ethical Response to Transsexual Persons" by Victoria Kolakowski in *Theology & Sexuality* (1997)

Come Home! Reclaiming Spirituality and Community as Gay Men and Lesbians (Second Edition, 1998) by Chris Glaser. Note: The "Safer Spirituality" chapter is not in the first edition.

"A Homoerotic Approach to Scripture" by Timothy Koch in *Theology and Sexuality* (2001)

Omnigender: A Trans-Religious Approach (2001 and 2007) by Virginia Ramey Mollenkott

Transgender Good News (2002) by Pat Conover

Trans-Gendered: Theology, Ministry, and Communities of Faith (2003 and 2018) by Justin Tanis

Transfigurations: Transgressing Gender in the Bible (theatrical production 2007–2016) by Peterson Toscano. Also available on DVD (2017)

"Practicing Safer Spirituality: Changing the Subject and Focusing on Justice" by Marvin Ellison in *Out of the Shadows, Into the Light: Christianity and Homosexuality* (2009), edited by Miguel A. De La Torre

"Transgressing Gender at Passover with Jesus!" by Peterson Toscano in *Gender Outlaws: The Next Generation* (2010) by Kate Bornstein and S. Bear Bergman

"'Josephine': Nov 9 @middlechurch" (2014) by J Mase III on YouTube (https://www.youtube.com/watch?v=qtE48ng6sL4)

Walking toward Resurrection: A Transgender Passion Narrative (2015) by Shannon T. L. Kearns (available from Queer Theology, http://www.queertheology.com)

Sex Difference in Christian Theology: Male, Female, and Intersex in the Image of God (2015) by Megan DeFranza

Understanding Gender Dysphoria: Navigating Transgender Issues in a Changing Culture (2015) by Mark Yarhouse

The Bible Tells Me So: Why Defending Scripture Has Made Us Unable to Read It (2015) by Peter Enns

"A Multi-Faith Theology on Moving beyond Intimate Partner Violence" (2016) by J Mase III (published by Believe Out Loud, http://www.believeoutloud.com)

Transforming: The Bible and the Lives of Transgender Christians (2018) by Austen Hartke

Bible Bash podcast, Episode 1 (2019), "The Creation of the Earth Being" by Liam Hooper and Peterson Toscano

And Then I Got Fired: One Transqueer's Reflections on Grief, Unemployment, and Inappropriate Jokes about Death (2019) by J Mase III. See also "Bad Theology: Or a Black Trans Man Attempts Salvation" (2018) on Yeni Sleidi's YouTube channel, for a stunning spoken word version.

Opening Plenary Panel, *Christianity and White Supremacy: Heresy and Hope Conference* (Princeton University, March 29, 2019, recording available at http://bit.ly/2N07bdv). More about the conference at http://bit.ly/2FjiTJK

Other Works Cited

Strong's Concordance with Hebrew and Greek Lexicon (1890 and later reprints)

The Souls of Black Folk (1903) by W. E. B. Du Bois

Making Sex: Body and Gender from the Greeks to Freud (1990) by Thomas Laqueur

"Either/Or—Neither/Both: Sexual Ambiguity and the Ideology of Gender" by Julia Epstein in *Genders* (1990)

"'No More Than a Boy': The Shifting Construction of Masculinity from Ancient Greece to the Middle Ages" by Jonathan Walters in *Gender & History* (1993)

"Starting Over" (unpublished sermon on Nicodemus) by Chris Paige (at Tabernacle United Church, Philadelphia, PA, 1999)

"The Lost One" (unpublished sermon on Judas) by Chris Paige (at Tabernacle United Church, Philadelphia, PA, 2000)

Unpublished sermon on the Beatitudes at a commitment ceremony by Patricia Pearce (at Tabernacle United Church, Philadelphia, PA, 2000)

"Terms Paradox" (Victim Service Providers' Fact Sheet #2, 2012) by FORGE

"A Gender Not Listed Here: Genderqueers, Gender Rebels, and OtherWise in the National Transgender Discrimination Survey" in *LGBTQ Policy Journal at the Harvard Kennedy School* (2012) by Jack Harrison, Jaime Grant, and Jody L. Herman

"A Personal History of the 'T-Word' (and some more general reflections on language and activism)" (2014) by Julia Serano (published at http://juliaserano.blogspot.com)

"Guidelines for Psychological Practice with Transgender and Gender Nonconforming People" (2015) by the American Psychological Association

Online review (2016) by Logan regarding *Crossing Over: Liberating the Transgendered Christian* (2002) by Vanessa Sheridan (collected by GoodReads, http://www.goodreads.org)

"AMA takes several actions supporting transgender patients" (2017) by Robert Nagler Miller (published on the American Medical Association website, http://www.ama-assn.org)

"Roundtable: Toward a Transfeminist Religious Studies" in *Journal of Feminist Studies in Religion* (2018) with Max Strassfeld, et al

Definition of "transgender" (published by Merriam Webster Online, https://www.merriam-webster.com)

Additional Note

A bibliography on sex and gender in indigenous cultures would need a book of its own to do justice to the many cultures and traditions around the world (and over time). Many popular early publications tend to reflect Western anthropological assumptions, which is problematic. Look for resources by representatives *from* the culture or tradition. Be careful considering resources that are by outsiders that are simply *about* the tradition.

Appendix A
Sexual Orientation and the Bible

Clobber Passages

Below are the Bible passages that are most prominently used to argue against same-gender-loving relationships:

Genesis 1 (see chapter 6 of OtherWise Christian)
Genesis 2 (see chapter 7 of OtherWise Christian)
Genesis 19
Leviticus 18:22 (mentioned in chapter 9 of OtherWise Christian)
Leviticus 20:13
Deuteronomy 23:17–18
Romans 1:26–27
I Corinthians 6:9
I Timothy 1:9–10
Jude 1:6–7

Recommended Resources

Over the last 50 years or so, many resources have been developed to deal with the sexual-orientation "clobber passages." The following organizations are trusted sources that may be useful in exploring affirming viewpoints among folk who take the Bible seriously:

The Reformation Project (http://www.reformationproject.org)
Queer Theology (http://www.queertheology.com)
Soulforce (http://www.soulforce.org)

For those of us who have been hurt by people who use the Bible as a weapon against same-gender-loving people, I also recommend *Steps to Recovery from Bible Abuse* (2000) by Rembert Truluck, because it addresses the topic with an eye toward healing.

Appendix B
Reading the Bible Again

Safer spirituality also means vetting resources. This list is a diverse array of books (in alphabetical order by author), each with its own perspective, but that are not specifically about OtherWise experience. These are just a few recommendations for those who want additional support as they dig deeper into the Bible as a source for resistance and liberation.

Razing Hell: Rethinking Everything You've Been Taught about God's Wrath and Judgment (2010) by Sharon L. Baker

Love Wins: A Book About Heaven, Hell, and the Fate of Every Person Who Ever Lived (2011) by Rob Bell

What Is the Bible? How an Ancient Library of Poems, Letters, and Stories Can Transform the Way You Think and Feel about Everything (2017) by Rob Bell

Meeting Jesus Again for the First Time: The Historical Jesus and the Heart of Contemporary Faith (1995 with later reprints) by Marcus Borg

*Reading the Bible Again for the First Time: Taking the Bible Seriously but Not Literally (*2001) by Marcus Borg

The Cross and the Lynching Tree (2011) James H. Cone

Reading the Bible from the Margins (2002) by Miguel de la Torre

"Breaking Open: Biblical Literalism & Inerrancy," edited by Alba de Onofrio, available at www.soulforce.org

Set Them Free: The Other Side of Exodus (2002) by Laurel Dykstra

Liberating Biblical Study: Scholarship, Art, and Action (2011), edited by Laurel Dykstra and Ched Myers

The Bible Tells Me So: Why Defending Scripture Has Made Us Unable to Read It (2015) by Peter Enns

How the Bible Actually Works: In Which I Explain How an Ancient, Ambiguous, and Diverse Book Leads Us to Wisdom Rather Than Answers—and Why That's Great News (2019) by Peter Enns

Inspired: Slaying Giants, Walking on Water, and Loving the Bible Again (2018) by Rachel Held Evans

Five Books of Miriam: A Woman's Commentary on the Torah (1997) by Ellen Frankel

Daughters of Miriam: Women Prophets in Ancient Israel (2008) by Wilda C. Gafney

Womanist Midrash: A Reintroduction to the Women of the Torah and the Throne (2017) by Wilda C. Gafney

Nahum, Habakkuk, Zephaniah (2017) by Wilda C. Gafney

The Good Book: Reading the Bible with Mind and Heart (2002) by Peter Gomes

Unsettling the Word: Biblical Experiments in Decolonization (2019), edited by Steve Heinrichs

Unveiling Empire: Reading Revelation Then and Now (1999) by Anthony Gwyther and Wes Howard-Brook

"Come Out My People!": God's Call Out of Empire in the Bible and Beyond (2010) by Wes Howard-Brook

Empire Baptized: How the Church Embraced What Jesus Rejected (2016) by Wes Howard-Brook

Living in the Shadow of the Cross: Understanding and Resisting the Power and Privilege of Christian Hegemony (2013) by Paul Kivel

The Misunderstood Jew: The Church and the Scandal of the Jewish Jesus (2009) by Amy-Jill Levine

Entering the Passion of Jesus: A Beginner's Guide to Holy Week (2018) by Amy-Jill Levine

The Jewish Annotated New Testament (2011), edited by Amy-Jill Levine and Marc Zvi Brettler

The Meaning of the Bible: What the Jewish Scriptures and Christian Old Testament Can Teach Us (2011) by Amy-Jill Levine and Douglas A. Knight

Binding the Strong Man: A Political Reading of Mark's Story of Jesus (1988) by Ched Myers

Who Will Roll Away the Stone? Discipleship Queries for First World Christians (1994) by Ched Myers

The Africana Bible: Reading Israel's Scriptures from Africa and the African Diaspora (2009), edited by Hugh R. Page Jr., et al.

Rescuing the Bible from Fundamentalism: A Bishop Rethinks the Meaning of Scripture (1992 and 2009) by John Shelby Spong

Liberating the Gospels: Reading the Bible with Jewish Eyes (2009) by John Shelby Spong

Jesus and the Disinherited (1984) by Howard Thurman

Steps to Recovery from Bible Abuse (2000) by Rembert Truluck

Just a Sister Away: Understanding the Timeless Connection between Women of Today and Women in the Bible (2007 revision of 1988 classic) by Renita J. Weems

I Asked for Intimacy: Stories of Blessings, Betrayals, and Birthings (1993) by Renita J. Weems

Battered Love: Marriage, Sex, and Violence in the Hebrew Prophets (1995) by Renita J. Weems

Some of these books will be available through your local library. Many are available at a steep discount through used book sellers online. Watch http://www.otherwisechristian.com for more detailed book reviews and additional ideas!

Appendix C
Christendom, White Bullshit, and the Power of Colonial Imagination

A warped theological imagination
has fed us a lie:
We own the table to which we invite others.
We are perpetual hosts.
Others are perpetual guests.
Hospitality is something we give,
rarely something we receive.

Eric Barreto
Opening Panel
Christianity and White Supremacy:
Heresy and Hope Conference

In *OtherWise Christian*, I have argued that we have all been bamboozled by this Western settler-colonial notion of sex and gender as having two and only two permanent and mutually exclusive "opposite" options as determined by biology at birth. My emphasis has been on Christian (and Jewish) tradition with a particular focus on biblical text. However, I also want to acknowledge that there exists a growing body of work in post-colonial studies which is also pertinent, though I am not well-positioned to summarize the field.

As I noted in chapter 2, modern gender oppression is closely connected to white supremacy and Christian supremacy. The *Christianity and White Supremacy: Heresy and Hope Conference* (XWS19) at Princeton University in March 2019 provided me with some potent ideas for further exploration. I will share some highlights here in the hopes that others will expand and elaborate on these beginning kernels of insight.

In the opening panel of the conference, Mark Charles argues provocatively that Christendom has rejected the teachings of Jesus, especially those about suffering and persecution. More specifically, when Eusebius of Caesarea recruited the Emperor Constantine to Christianity, the "heresy of Christian empire" emerged. Charles argues that the Christendom project embraced power, wealth, and prosperity in a way that is antithetical to Jesus' teaching. He accuses church fathers, including Augustine and later Aquinas, of advancing this heresy by arguing in favor of using the power and resources of the (now Christian) empire to compel others to follow the teachings of the church. In other words, the Christian state would be ordained to cause fear, punishment, and pain in Jesus' name, while the Church at Rome would become a political apparatus seeking control of hearts and minds by means of violence and coercion.

This Christendom project led to the Council of Nicea (325 CE) and other efforts to standardize Christian teaching. At this critical juncture, Christianity shifted decisively away from multivocal testimony—from being a loose collection of Gospels, letters, teachers, and communities—toward being a closed canon and a master narrative of one (dominant and domineering) faith. It is one thing to say "I follow this teacher" or "I prefer this text." It is quite another to employ state violence as a means to eliminate competing points of view. Naming heretics became a way to consolidate power.

Charles further connects these shifts to centuries of European colonization through the Doctrine of Discovery, which became the basis for land grants in the U.S. The heresy of Christendom also infected the Protestant Reformation. Charles argues, "American exceptionalism is rooted in the lie of white supremacy which is a fruit of the heresy of Christian empire" (Charles, XWS19 opening). In summary, he claims that Christendom is a "rejection of the teaching of Jesus" and an embrace of "a narrative of prosperity."

The opening panel of the conference addresses "the [Christian] tradition" as a problem. Yolanda Pierce points out, "Tradition is how a people, a body, encounter[s] the text and live[s] out that text in relationship with each other and the Divine" (Pierce, XWS19 opening). She argues that the pervasiveness of a dominant tradition is part of its power—that maintaining the dominant narrative requires people, rituals, text or interpretation of texts, and other common denominators, which become the vernacular within which we discuss any and all problems that may emerge. Andrew Wymer contributes, "Tradition is a manifestation of power" (Wymer, XWS19 opening). The panel acknowledges that there are actually multiple traditions, but that the one aligned with Christian empire, colonization, and white supremacy is particularly dominant.

Eric Barreto speaks about the power of the colonial imagination. While it is convenient to blame the most egregious of humanitarian violations in Christendom on political and secular powers, Barreto argues that the colonial imagination has "wormed its way into our lives through preaching and prayer, the reading of scripture, and the parceling out of grace" (Barreto, XWS19 opening). He argues that we have a theological crisis because our churches have

> cast a biblical and ethical imagination that has shriveled our capacities to love our neighbors near and far... [Our leaders] have fed a colonial imagination more concerned with ownership... [than] grace, power more than partnership, acquisition more than curiosity... Colonial imagination in the tradition has taught us that the peoples of the world are means not ends—that people and their lands are only as valuable as the goods they can produce for the colonial center. Colonial imagination has taught us that it is better to be right than to be loving. Colonial imagination has taught us that biblical interpretation is an act of grasping, of ownership, of claiming readings of scripture as singular and as right and as universal because they are mine and mine alone. (Baretto, XWS19 opening)

We have not only been bamboozled about gender. We have been bamboozled about race and religion more generally. In the same plenary, Wymer provides an academically-informed introduction to "white bullshit." He defines white bullshit as "any public or private words, gestures, or postures that intentionally or unintentionally direct attention away from the ongoing creation and maintenance of systems of whiteness and the potential subversion and eradication of white supremacy" (Wymer, XWS19 opening). White bullshit is a distraction from what matters and Wymer speaks to the ways that white Christian traditions serve as a significant source of white bullshit.

Citing G. A. Cohen, Wymer notes that bullshit is a deceptive process, something that is socially fluid and that changes. We can be caught up in bullshit and we may not even know we are caught up in it! According to Wymer, there is an impulse to maintain the tension between maintaining the "violently gained benefits of white supremacy" and maintaining the "illusion of white purity and innocence." He says, "In order to maintain that contradiction, we need to bullshit ourselves and others, whether consciously or unconsciously, whether intentionally or unintentionally" (Wymer, XWS19 opening).

Such shenanigans around religion and politics are not unrelated to our discussion of sex and gender. The power dynamics of colonization require a rigorous means for determining who does or does not have access to land, wealth, opportunity, and power. Therefore, the regulation of reproduction, marriage, and inheritance becomes a key contribution to the maintenance of the colonial project, whether that is Christendom or American exceptionalism. It is not coincidental that it was under Constantine's Christendom project that the eunuch church father, Origen, was declared a heretic (see chapter 17).

Just as eunuchs of old would be demoted from citizens to foreigners, the citizenship of OtherWise-gendered people remains conditional in Christendom. In "Throwing a Party: Patriarchy, Gender, and the Death of Jezebel," Victoria Kolakowski warns us about the dangers of assimilation (see chapter 16). We must be vigilant about the ways that colonial projects will ask us to align ourselves not only with toxic masculinity but also with white supremacy and Christendom more generally.

Jesus showed solidarity with eunuchs as a way to be clear about zir allegiances (see chapter 14). Ebed-melech and the traveler in Acts 8 were not just eunuchs—they were Ethiopian eunuchs, slaves, and foreigners (see chapter 15). Paul's proclamations were not just about gender but also about religion, race, and class (chapter 22). Let us not be fooled by white bullshit or vaunted promises from an emperor. Transgender liberation must not sidestep issues of race, class, and religion.

Baretto argues that we have "inherited and then consumed a marred theological imagination" (Baretto, XWS19 opening). I would add that the two-and-only-two gender model is a part of that perverted theological imagination—a warped view of the world in which OtherWise-gendered people, such as Jesus (see chapter 14) and the Ethiopian eunuch (see chapter 15), are either erased from memory or robbed of their revolutionary power. Christendom asks OtherWise-gendered folk to forget our truest selves in order to be "perfect servants" (see chapter 11) of the empire, but scripture reminds us that God and God alone "will give us an everlasting name that will endure forever" (Isaiah 56:5b, see chapter 13).

I am not interested in defending whether OtherWise-gendered people are God's children. The scriptures are clear and our lives testify to our value for those who will receive it (referencing Matthew 19:12 and John 3:11, see chapter 25 and 23 respectively). What hope is there in being citizens of Christendom—of a Christian empire that has already rejected Jesus? Instead, I want nothing less than to ignite the OtherWise imagination of the church, so we can better join in the resistance against the powers and principalities of our age (Ephesians 6:12).

Where do you land in the colonial imagination? Are you a perpetual host, responsible for judging others? Or have others rendered you an unwanted guest who needs to wait for a proper invitation? Have you been adopted by the "House of Jesus" (see chapter 25)? Are you being recruited to the militia or the armed forces of Christendom? Would you follow a refugee (see chapter 23) or convicted criminal (see chapter 25), like Zey Jesus? Are you caught up in the white bullshit of the Christian emperors of our day? How are you responding to the revolutionary invitation of this OtherWise-gendered teacher from the Middle East?

Appendix D
Poetry Is Not A Luxury

Poetry is not only dream and vision;
it is the skeleton architecture
of our lives.
It lays the foundations
for a future of change,
a bridge across our fears
of what has never been before.

Audre Lorde, 1984
excerpt from "Poetry Is Not a Luxury"

Agape: For My Elders

By Chris Paige, 1999

Know What was Born(e) here.
Love.

Hold on to what you know.
Life.

Follow your dreams.
Speak your visions.
Your children are alive
and fighting
to survive.

Grateful for the dream.
Joy.

But still looking for home.
Longing.

Do not settle for wandering in the wilderness
When the promised land is close at hand.
Your children are listening.

I am OtherWise

By Chris Paige, 2015

I am OtherWise. I am male and female. Neither. Both. I have been given a non-binary gender. Made in the image of an OtherWise God (Genesis) who transcends labels. "I am who I am."

I am OtherWise. I honor the courage and strength of my two spirit siblings, who struggle to reclaim their traditional places in Native circles: *winkté*, *nádleehí*, and more.

I am OtherWise. I acknowledge that it was settler-colonists, invader-immigrants from Europe who came with rigid and binary ideas about gender. Enforcing those ideas on indigenous peoples in the Americas through violence and cultural genocide. Labeling my two spirit siblings as evil and feeding them, literally, to the dogs of war.

I am OtherWise. Those European settler-invaders were Christians, funded by church people. The tools of gendered violence had already been used for many generations in the Old Country to eliminate the OtherWise—gender non-conforming people, as well as Pagans, wise women, healers, and other so-called heretics and perverts who challenged the status quo.

I am OtherWise. I hear the voices of the slaughtered still crying out from those "burning years." The genocide of my own tribe long before Columbus "sailed the ocean blue." Demons unleashed again in the middle passage, residential schools, internment camps... and so many other places from Ferguson, Missouri, to Kampala, Uganda.

I am OtherWise. I am a witness to the resurrection. All of this is my heritage and inheritance. Jesus calling for our demons be cast out. Jesus inviting us to rise again from these tombs of our own making. Born again.

I am OtherWise. My pronouns are they/them.

Acknowledgements

Any book is more than the work of the author;
it is also a composite of the work,
experience, and generosity
of many minds.

Judy Grahn
Another Mother Tongue: Gay Words, Gay Worlds
acknowledgements, page xvii

OtherWise Christian is definitely a "composite" book, because it surveys, compiles, and shares the work of so many others in the field. Many resources have been cited and I want to begin my acknowledgements by thanking that cloud of witnesses—authors and scholars who have poured themselves into their work and, thus, indirectly into mine. I hope that you will be proud to be a part of *OtherWise Christian* and that you will feel my gratitude.

In addition, I want to honor three OtherWise prophets, specifically: Leslie Feinberg who imagined a thing called, "Trans Liberation," Kate Bornstein who showed us how to be a "Gender Outlaw," and Audre Lorde, sister outsider, who dared speak of our power. These three were OtherWise resistance leaders before I knew what resistance was, and I believe that their influence will be felt for many generations to come.

As a transgender-identified person of faith, I needed a community of seekers who could reflect my experience of gender and spirit. Such community was not easy to find at first, but a rag-tag bunch of us found one another and we ended up building, first a website, then an organization called Transfaith (http://www.transfaith.info). This book would not be possible without that diverse community of individuals and the collective energies that have been raised through our work together. While listing specific names would inevitably leave out precious friends and colleagues, I do want to specifically thank Ovid Amorson for so magically breaking through the white bullshit to shine a magical light on all that matters most.

While it is now defunct, *The Other Side* magazine was my first job out of college, and the community around the magazine introduced me to an ecumenical array of justice-minded travelers who profoundly impacted the way that I understand the Christian Bible—no one more important than my beloved friend, Elizabeth Terry. I also learned a lot about publishing and non-profit management.

Two local, Philadelphia faith communities have adopted and claimed me in ways that have shaped my journey profoundly. Tabernacle United Church welcomed a quirky 20-something college graduate who was new to town in 1994. Living Water United Church of Christ (repeatedly) welcomed an older, more cynical, but still quirky adoptive parent. Both communities have been touchstones in my adult life and the source of endless comfort, for which I am deeply grateful.

The profound impact that Daniel Foor's teaching has had on me will be felt more than seen in this work. In particular, his teaching has helped me to begin to claim the multiple lineages that have shaped my ministry and witness.

John Linscheid was an openly gay man and biblical scholar at *The Other Side* magazine before I could even imagine why such a thing would matter. His efforts were ground-breaking and remain too often overlooked. I am grateful to call him an elder and a friend.

Sister Merry Peter and Ken White became mothers and midwives to me in ways I did not know that I needed. I claim the Sisters of Perpetual Indulgence as my OtherWise kin. I am grateful to my fairie and Komo family for holding me with gentleness, ferocity, and joy in years when I was barely beginning to understand what conjuring OtherWise is all about.

While I no longer identify as a woman, the rowdy sisterhood of CLOUT, Christian Lesbians Out Together, taught me to love myself and to believe in myself. I like to call Janie Spahr my homiletics professor, because this baby dyke learned so much following zem around and Janie never turned me away or shamed me for it. I am a disciple of Carter Heyward and credit her theological probing of the power of relationship as deeply influential on who I have become. I am grateful to Irene Monroe and Tolonda Henderson for graciously providing wisdom, insight, and friendship, each in their own way, as I began to emerge from nice, white, liberal levels of racial awareness. I am also grateful to count Melanie Morrison as a mentor and a friend. White allies need white allies. I highly recommend Melanie's *Doing Our Own Work: An Anti Racism Workshop for White People* program (https://www.alliesforchange.org) as a powerful resource for white people who want to do better. There are so many more precious names, but I will risk naming just a few beloved elders: Beverly Harrison, Virginia Mollenkott, Nancy Krody, Mary Hunt. Thank you, sister-siblings, one and all.

In many ways, Bishop Yvette Flunder together with the Fellowship of Affirming Ministries and the TransSaints family opened a door for me to begin to get to know a whole other part of Christianity, spirituality, and my own vocation—not least of all by introducing me to this Louis Mitchell character. I am grateful to count Jonathon Thunderword as an elder and a friend. I knew that I loved her, but I didn't realize how much Mother Major

Griffin-Gracy reminded me of Jesus until I wrote chapter 25! Risen ancestors, Bobbie Jean Baker and Charlene Arcila, you will not be forgotten. I call your names. Each of you has taught me in your own way about perseverance, wisdom, and love. Thank you.

Words cannot convey the debt of gratitude I have for the many ways that Louis Mitchell and Johnny Manzon-Santos nourished my resilience in world-weary seasons when I might have laid it all down. They have begged, pleaded, encouraged, invited, cajoled, and demanded my voice. They have reminded me of OtherWisdom in times when my own despair has gotten in the way. You are cherished friends, beloved brothers, OtherWise kindred.

Thank you to Tolonda Henderson, Deborah Ahrens, Deb Burnham, and Liam Hooper for support related to my research for this book. Thank you to early readers, Louis Mitchell, Liam Hooper, Bobbi Taylor, Mykal Shannon, Ron Paige, and Carolyn Paige, who encouraged me to keep going and offered feedback. Thank you to Enzi Tanner, Joy Ladin, Nick Manchester, Peterson Toscano, J Mase III, Z Shane Zaldivar, and Upāsikā tree for additional insights and suggestions. Thank you to Nancy Krody for expert copy-editing advice. Thank you to Dezjorn Gauthier for my author headshot.

This book is my new baby, but, Nevaeh Paige, you will always be my best thing ever. Suzanne Muench, thank you for surviving with me all of these years. Nana and Gina and all my adopted family, you mean the world to me. Last but not least, I am grateful to my parents, Carolyn and Ron Paige, for their endless, unconditional love and for their tangible support both in life and in launching OtherWise Engaged Publishing. I still "love you for the whole world" and now the whole world can read about it. I pray that the witness of *OtherWise Christian* will make all of you proud.

♡

♡

There are many kinds of power, used and unused, acknowledged or [OtherWise].

Audre Lorde, "Uses of the Erotic: The Erotic as Power"

[The U.S.] is aggressively trying to enforce this radically fundamentalist, racist, classist, and all-the-rest-ists version of the world, which could [OtherWise] be a decent Judeo-Christian system of values, ethics, and morality.

Kate Bornstein, *My New Gender Workbook*

But believe me, honey, you're not alone in the feeling that you're not a man or a woman. ... You're more than just neither, honey. There's other ways to be than either-or. It's not so simple. [OtherWise] there wouldn't be so many people who don't fit.

Leslie Feinberg, *Stone Butch Blues*

♡

About the Author

Chris Paige is an OtherWise-identified writer, educator, organizer, and coach (https://chrispaige.com). Chris was founding executive director of Transfaith (http://www.transfaith.info), a multi-tradition, multi-racial, multi-gender advocacy organization by and for people of transgender experience. Previously, Chris had been publisher and co-director of the (now defunct) award-winning progressive Christian magazine, *The Other Side.*

CPSIA information can be obtained
at www.ICGtesting.com
Printed in the USA
LVHW031501121219
640281LV00013B/985/P